Sustainable Development

Possible with Creative System Engineering

by
Walter Sobkiw

Published by

C~B
CassBeth, Cherry Hill, NJ

Courtesy National Science Foundation

1. Letter Of Transmittal
2. President Roosevelt's Letter
3. Science The Endless Frontier, A Report to the President by Vannevar Bush, Director of the Office of Scientific Research and Development, July 1945 (United States Government Printing Office, Washington: 1945)

Published by Cassbeth, Cherry Hill, New Jersey, USA

For information contact www.cassbeth.com

First Edition

Library of Congress Control Number: 2008904255

ISBN: 978-0-6152-1630-0

I would like to thank everyone
that allowed me to get to this point.

This especially holds for my wife and children
who have allowed me to pursue my callings,
which eventually led me to this path.

Preface

There is no secret alien space technology, there is only us, and we have to make the best of what we have or we will fight for what little is available. Science, Innovation, Technology, and Engineering - SITE - are what have allowed the human population to increase in our 5000 plus years of civilization. It is SITE that maximizes the use of our natural resources. If we fall down in this area our only alternatives are war, revolution, and genocide as famine and want grip a naturally increasing human population.

So this little book is a wakeup call. It makes the statement that our SITE is breaking down just when we need it to ramp up. The best way to describe it is we are all now aware of sustainable development, but few realize that sustainable development has always been part of human development and that it was our SITE and how effectively it worked which allowed for sustainable development of previous generations. From crop rotation farming to automobile junkyards to what needs to happen in the next 100 years.

This book is an attempt to go back to our fundamentals of Science, Innovation, Technology, Engineering and Art. Our organizations are sick and not capable of the challenges that must be addressed in our rapidly approaching future. In fact, since Word War II we have eliminated many organizations that may need to be recreated, if possible, if we ever hope to address these challenges.

This book is intended to be thin, so it can be read in one sitting. However, its content should spur thinking and postulating and offer some simple rules to kick our failing SITE in the ass. If it fails then you give it a try, build from this work.

Introduction

So what is this book about: sustainable development or creative system engineering. The answer is both. We humans are facing the greatest challenge in our 5000 plus years of civilization. That challenge is to figure out how to make it through the next 100 years and reject the temptation of killing off billions of humans so that there is enough left over for the few survivors.

I will make the claim that the only way we can do this is through the application of Creative System Engineering. There are no governments, institutions, companies, management techniques, political dogma, ideologies or other engineering scientific or technical approaches that will get us through the next 100 years of peaceful sustainable development.

I will also make the claim that Creative System Engineering is not new and was practiced extensively after WWII and yielded our modern world of water, sewage, electricity, telephones, radios, televisions, airplanes, cars, dishwashers, highways. The problem is we forgot how to do Creative System Engineering. We did not name it we just did it.

What is Creative System Engineering? Imagine a place where you create things and make decisions where there are no hidden agendas and all stakeholders are treated equally. How would potential approaches surface, how would they be narrowed and selected, how would decisions be made. What tools and techniques would be used if they were not the greatest moneyed interests, the most politically powerful, or the most dangerous?

How about the scientific method using reasonable techniques understood by reasonable people in a process that is fully transparent and visible to everyone. Everyone has a view of all the alternatives. Everyone has a view of all the decision paths. Everyone has an opportunity to impact the alternatives and decision paths. Do not fall for the rhetoric that this is mob rule or design by committee. These are reasonable people using 5000 plus years of tools,

1

techniques, processes, and methods to make informed decisions. There are no hidden agendas with vested interests or people who just give up and go silent or worse compromise. Everyone is comfortable with the decision because it is intuitively obvious to all. Everyone obviously has responsibility in such an endeavor. No one can blow off that responsibility.

That in a nutshell is Creative System Engineering. This book hopefully will provide the framework for us to start practicing this "dying" art.

Creative System Engineering is not new. Education, Science, and Engineering were the pillars that were used to create a spectacular world after WWII. These pillars literally allowed us to go to the Moon. The great system engineering projects were all implemented with massive internal education, massive new science, and massive new engineering. This resulted in creative system solutions that changed our world forever. The genie was let out of the bottle and the world has never been the same. This simple book just applied the word Creative to System Engineering to represent the previous century technique used on system engineering programs that changed our world for the better in ways we can not imagine. All we can do is look back in amazement.

Bachelor of Science

Typically system engineers come from engineering degrees like electrical engineering. They sometimes come from the sciences like physics. They have a good background in the general sciences like physics, chemistry, mathematics and general engineering principles like mechanics, electricity, and chemistry. They then specialize in either mechanical, electrical, chemical, civil, biological or other engineering areas. When they leave the university they then get exposed to other science and technology views and methods. This is a list of some of the more important aspects of engineering.

The funny thing is that many people without a formal education in engineering or science can relate to and understand these items. This is where it gets interesting, because these people can and should have stakeholder status in major science and engineering efforts. So this list not only expands the traditional specialists' view but it also allows the inclusion of the non-specialist into the process. So this is a list of items with brief comments and descriptions. Everyone can relate to this list and when they engage they can use these brief comments, descriptions, and lessons as a guide.

Systems Thinking

What better way to start this book than with a message post I wrote about system thinking?

--- Prior to your post I was seriously considering "unplugging" from this "message board" or mirror. The topics and discussions lacked relevance for me and clogged my mailbox with noise. Also there is no history or anonymity, like on a traditional message board. If that mechanism were in place I could look at previous posts (2 years ago) and perhaps find some relevance. I also think more people would post in such an anonymous environment. I hope the message board comes up soon. . . Anyway, to my response.

Your post takes me back to where I "was introduced to system engineering", Hughes Aircraft. In that time and place I was introduced to "systems thinking" and immediately realized its power. By the way they had 2,000 people in the systems division at Ground Systems Group. Since then I have come to realize that others know of this power and typically subvert and marginalize it and its practitioners. However, the part of Hughes I was associated with addressed only problems (national and international) no one else would tackle. They would pride themselves on always providing a real working solution. So IMHO (in my humble opinion), "systems thinking" is one of the most powerful forms of thinking known to humans. It is also very dangerous to some people. That is why it can be applied to problems no one will touch with a 10 foot pole, but fails on what should be simple things. . . I will explain further. . .

Since I left Hughes I have only seen "systems" advertised and marginalized as hidden agendas with outside and internal influences were allowed to negatively affect the "solutions". Most organizations pay lip service to the topic and are driven by lower level forces, usually a hidden stakeholder with enormous power whose only goal is financial or a promotion in the organization. It was over 20 years ago when I was making my rounds interviewing for another position when I spoke with someone who stood out from above the crowd in every way. He made the statement that there are only 5 companies in the USA that know and practice "system engineering". Hughes was on that list. That list is now smaller and may no longer be valid if those organization capitulated to "management".

Today we see some big problems facing our world. I think you are correct that "systems thinking" can help solve these problems. I think people from the previous generation used systems thinking to get them out of the death spiral of economic depression and WWII. However, there are powerful forces with hidden agendas that will do everything under the sun to subvert and in the end marginalize the "systems" approach. There are many people that have been spun out of the "Hughes like entities" and find themselves, alone, in other organizations with "system hostile" characteristics. Most of these people have left "systems", but some have stayed and tried to help these organizations, usually at great cost. So step A is for "systems people" to realize the threats and establish a "system" to protect the *"systems approach".*

Now here is a dirty little secret. Most organizations engaged heavily in system engineering were the Aerospace and Defense companies, both of which were heavily subsidized by taxpayers in the last century. In fact Hughes Aircraft was a non profit entity. So how do you measure and encourage progress if it's not driven by the bottom line or the buddy network? As you start to go down this "thought exercise"; you will then realize why "systems thinking" is so dangerous to some people in positions of power. Back in the 90's I addressed these topics with a mechanical engineer that started at IBM, went to a "lower level company", then went into business. He made the profound statement that it was about "self image". He said IBM would specifically ferret out people with low self-esteem, so that the problem solving would not be perverted. That sounded like a "management" solution to protect some aspect of "systems thinking".

Anyway, this technical organization can become a great organization, but it will involve great risk. It is at the very heart of some of these issues and unless they are addressed with some "great minds" using "systems thinking" we will continue to see problems on our small planet get worse. So yes, there is a huge role and challenge for this organization and it is not all engineering!

On the lighter side, some fields traditionally associated with reductionism are starting to look into the "systems approach". One example is in the bio sciences field and cancer research where the whole-body is being addressed and studied as a system. This work is at the University level. . . with funding from the Howard Hughes Medical Institute. . . hum. . .---

So what is Systems Thinking? I hope that this book will introduce you to system thinking and move you into the ranks of those practitioners. The reality is many of us engage in systems thinking in our everyday lives when we reject fate and try to control our destinies. We use whatever tools we have at our disposal to make these decisions every day of our lives. That is why this book is for everyone. Everyone engaged in our modern world should have some say in its evolution and that say should be from the system perspective of their view. So we can start at this point by saying that System Thinking has the following key elements:

1. You always broaden your horizons and perspective. Just when you think you have it, move to a broader view.
2. You reject the status quo. If you find yourself in that mix, step out of it and look for truth. It takes time for a valid solution to solidify.
3. You reject all vested interests including hidden interests.
4. You try to see the forest from the trees but always zoom in onto the leaf of a particular tree and find the cute bug sitting on the edge.
5. You should not fall into the trap of being set only at one abstraction level, the high level. You must be able to scale all abstraction levels simultaneously. This is hard.

I hope you enjoy the rest of the book.

Tradeoffs

The most important aspect of the tradeoff study is not the results but the journey. It is during the journey that the stakeholders learn things about the alternatives and ramifications of those alternatives that would normally never surface. Many people try to complicate the tradeoff study because they attempt to document the journey without realizing they are documenting the journey. Once that simple realization sinks in then the documented journey is a pleasure to read and understand.

In the beginning of a trade study there is nothing, just a blank sheet of paper. The first step is to identify alternatives, no matter how bizarre. One of the alternatives should be the current approach. List the alternatives and create 2 additional columns and label them advantages and disadvantages. This is basically the Benjamin Franklin method of decision-making that I was taught in elementary school in; you guessed it, Philadelphia. Keep this on a single sheet of paper so you can visualize it and cut to the key issues. It is easy to get lost in the noise. This also quickly cuts down on the alternatives. If you only have 2 alternatives something is wrong. If you have 10 alternatives something is wrong. The answer is in between and should include the impossible alternatives.

The advantages-disadvantages or plusses-minuses tables are very important. It is at this time that the key tradeoff criteria start to surface. These tradeoff criteria will be used in the next phase of the trade study. At this point we depart the Benjamin Franklin method and start moving into the heart of system engineering.

Identify your tradeoff criteria in rows and list your alternatives as columns. In the beginning of the trade study try to fill in each cell of the matrix using high medium low or numbers of 1 to 10 or 1 to 3 or 1 to 4. Literally play with each approach. You do this in one day. Now comes the hard part. Look at each criteria and architecture alternative. Look at each intersection or cell. Now start to identify studies techniques methods approaches from 5000 plus years of civilization to convert those initial gut-based ratings into ratings backed by sound scientific and engineering principles.

This process may take years. Take snapshots and change the cells of the tradeoff matrix. Add weights to the criteria based on your continued refined analysis of the problem. Some criteria may disappear and others may surface. Don't be afraid to call the team in and have everyone enter their view of the rating for each cell, no matter how detached they may be from the detailed studies. At some point some criteria become a wash while others become very different. Don't be afraid to perform a sensitivity analysis. This sensitivity analysis can fold into the tradeoff matrix. At some point the studies start to reach a level of diminishing returns and an approach starts to surface.

What should your tradeoff criteria include? That is really your call. It is part of the discovery process. However a word of caution. The tradeoff criteria should not include cost or requirements. It is a given that all solutions will satisfy the known requirements at some cost. Cost should be used at the bottom of the tradeoff where each approach total rating is divided by cost. This essentially identifies the goodness of each approach per unit of cost. This is called the measure of effectiveness or MOE.

MOE = Sum of tradeoff criteria/cost to produce approach

This is a terrifying experience for those who want control and have hidden agendas. Traditional management hates this. Vested interests both visible and hidden hate this. This is the heart of being System Engineering driven and there is management that understands this process and knows how to effectively manage it, but these managers are born only is system engineering driven organizations. This process is based on truth and it is fully transparent so that everyone understands the science and engineering, even the grandparents of the participants. That means that the studies and tradeoffs need to be communicated so that all stakeholders quickly grasp everything. This requires real genius.

At this point I recommend everyone investigate a technique invented at Hughes Aircraft Fullerton in the early 1960's. The technique is called STOP (Sequential Thematic Organization of Proposals). In the beginning it was applied to proposals, by the 80's it was being applied to studies that were extremely important to the nation and the world.

This is such an important topic I have restated it in the following paragraphs and I don't hold back any punches. This is key to our survival in the next century.

People will claim the MOE in many areas but the MOE is actually a measure of goodness per unit cost. That is a heavy statement, because it removes cost from the decision and yet considers cost.

You identify all of your criteria used in making a decision, like selecting the ideal architecture. Weigh and total the criteria for each approach trying to use formal analysis to backup the results. Now divide the total for each approach by the expected cost to develop that approach. So:

Sum of tradeoff criteria / cost to produce approach = MOE

This is extremely powerful and rails against recent trends and the rise of management in dictating decisions. The MOE is based on reason by reasonable people - - - using all the techniques of 5000+ years of civilization.

So the decision process is leveled and requested from the people using hard core scientific principles of analysis when possible, then processed either formally or informally (early in the process) using the MOE.

This is anathema to what has risen in the past 20+ years where decisions are abdicated to autocratic management usually driven by self interest (loaded words).

So system engineering is a process for solving problems using system engineers (always more than 1 in a true system engineering based effort). The system engineers "herd" all the stakeholders (hardware, software, mechanical, civil, chemical, maintenance, training, support, etc) so that all the criteria can be vetted and a reasonable decision can be made by reasonable people always using the MOE. This is like F=MA in physics. It is fundamental - it drives everything.

Most organizations reject system engineering for this reason. I would say we had 6 system engineering companies in the USA circa 1981. Today I am not sure we have any system engineering companies left standing. But that is a different topic.

The system engineering grand unifying equation: MOE = Sum of tradeoff criteria / cost to produce approach. This is how I was taught system engineering at a place that no longer exists - Hughes Aircraft.

Alternatives

Where do alternatives come from? That is a loaded question. Alternatives come from two primary areas. The first is from current and similar approaches. The second comes from humans. We try to define this unique human quality as creativity, innovation, and invention.

How many humans are involved in identifying alternatives? Well more than one! It does not matter how simple or complex the problem. If there is only one human identifying alternatives the organization is dysfunctional and the human has an extremely large ego.

The best way to describe this is through the concept of metrics. More or less 1 human is packed with 100 units of creativity, innovation, and invention - an IQ (invention quotient - the pun is intended) of lets say 100. There is probably no way to measure IQ, but if you could measure IQ and compare different humans it probably would not differ by more than a factor of 10, pick a number. Let's face it, living and surviving everyday is a very creative process. So you could have 1 human identifying alternatives or 1000 humans identifying alternatives.

Now it gets really interesting. At what point do the addition of more humans result in no new identification of alternatives? That is an interesting question. In an organizational setting you could start with 3 humans, let them identify alternatives, then start adding more humans over time. At some point diminishing returns start to surface. At some point gestalt surfaces and the IQ of the sum of humans gets a multiple. So 10 normal humans might result in an IQ of not 1000 but perhaps 100,000 a nice factor of 10.

How many alternatives should you consider? Well more than one! If you only have one alternative you are not engaged in a meaningful activity. Two is not the right answer either. That is normally a sign of someone stacking the solutions towards a vested interest.

Individuals who have more than two children know that the universe has more than two opposites. Somehow in the wonder and complexity of the universe the first two children are opposite and when the third child arrives that child is opposite the first two children. Those who have multiple pets make the same observations.

So the universe is more complex than left right, up down, centralized distributed, etc. The issue surfaces when you are engaged in a true system engineering effort and you are really trying to apply science and engineering principles to each alternative. That costs money. At some point pruning needs to happen in the early studies so that when the serious studies begin not only are costs controlled but also the stakeholders can actually follow the science and engineering. The number 7 plus / minus 2 is the answer. Eventually like in a horse race there are 2 competing alternatives.

Now for a really frightening observation!

Any of the latter stage alternatives can be made to work. One alternative might be strong in one area and weak in another area. Money can be applied to address the weak area. Each alternative will display this result and each alternative will cost about the same in the end.

This is an extremely powerful observation, and shakes true engineers and scientists engaged in these activities to the core. It usually surfaces in the heat of battle of selecting system architectures.

So why go through the process? Why not pick an alternative

using one human and just make it work? Well the alternative from the one human may not have made the short list once understood by the gestalt because of a fatal flaw. Also the weaknesses of the alternative will not be known. A weakness may surface when least expected and throw the whole project off the cliff or worse an operational catastrophe may kill millions of people.

Information Chunking

Chunking is a principle that applies to the effective communication of information. It is very important in written communication. In 1950 George A. Miller published a landmark journal article entitled "The Magical Number Seven, Plus or Minus Two". He studied short-term memory trying to determine how many numbers people could reliably remember a few minutes after having been told these numbers only once. The answer was: "The Magical Number Seven, Plus or Minus Two".

This concept applies in all forms of communications. It even applies to engineering activities such as software, where chunking reduces complexity by increasing understandability, which increases maintainability. Modularization was a big trend in the 1970s and it transformed many things from television sets to major infrastructure systems. Yourdons' famous structured system analysis from the 1970s was based on this finding.

The old term was called a rat's nest. This was typically a thing that did not represent or embrace the concept of chunking. There are still examples where people are not familiar with this work even though they have been exposed to outlining techniques in writing and structured system analysis techniques. Usually this is a sign of a problem in the organization where the solution was never really fully understood and yet a milestone needed to be met as mandated by management. So there is more to chunking than meets the eye.

Architecture

Architectures should be beautiful. They should raise goose pimples. They should be elegant, simple, and symmetric. Architectures should be well understood by everyone. Architectures should be characterized by science and engineering in studies. These studies should use any and all techniques from 5000 plus years or civilization. New architectures require new scientific and engineering processes, tools, and techniques. Architectures should be born from the fire of tradeoff and alternatives from people seeking truth.

Patterns are fleeting and change with time and the challenges. Operational people tend to think in terms of patterns. As subject matter experts they tend to bring the current system into the new architecture. They naturally resist new patterns because they feel they are unproven.

By definition state-of-the-art has few patterns and true innovation or beyond state-of-the-art has no patterns. Now a very important observation, humans find patterns. Humans find patterns where no patterns exist. It is fundamental to the way in which humans solve problems. So patterns are fundamental to solutions and all its studies, but the patterns should be new otherwise only previous state-of-the-art is being duplicated, which may be ok.

System Boundary

It is critical to establish the system context. This is the boundary that defines the system. Draw it on a piece of paper and label the inputs and outputs. Explain why the system boundary is the system boundary. If you are given a system boundary convince yourselves the system boundary is valid. If it is not the correct system boundary, then fix it. Always include the system boundary and its rationale with all discussions and presentations of the system architecture.

Prototypes

Physical models in R&D labs were replaced with software models were replaced with paper models were replaced with downsizing - please see yourself out the door we don't want to know the details. That has been the progression from the 1980's into the next century. The markets and natural selection were viewed as more effective than Research and Development. The price has been enormous and applied R&D died in the United States. There were great corporate labs that no longer exist and will be impossible to reproduce.

This trend started about the time the Federal Aviation Administration decided to start rolling out various prototypes from their internal and corporate R&D labs into the infrastructure. Instead the NAS Brown Book was created which merged these R&D efforts into large programs that required huge corporate consortiums to support.

The sad part is that the old formula of evolving prototypes that eventually make it to infrastructure now have a fancy name called incremental development and concurrent engineering. Except the old formula was still more successful than incremental development and concurrent engineering which has yet to prove it can create the spectacular systems created after WWII and peaking in the late 1960's. There used to be all types of prototypes. Here is just a partial list:

1. Research and Development prototypes
2. Proof of concept prototypes
3. Simulation labs that emulated possible solutions
4. Engineering models
5. Pre-production prototypes
6. Production prototypes

Everyone in everyday life applies the principles of prototypes.

Studies

Studies formalize the tradeoffs. They are where science and engineering lift the discussion from speculation, vested interests, dirt, and confusion. The studies are key to everything about the effort. All the studies should contain a summary so that anyone anywhere can understand the findings. This is where transparency is offered so that reasonable people can make reasonable decisions in that tradeoff matrix.

Studies surface the key requirements. These key requirements get moved into the specifications that will be used to implement one of the alternatives. The key requirements are just that, they are the system drivers. The driver can be technology, performance, cost, complexity, etc. Surfacing key requirements is an art and a difficult concept to initially grasp. It can only be learned by example and trial and error, as critical thinking abilities in true architecture people are able to home in on the key system drivers, the key requirements.

Modeling

A model is not about fancy equations and complex math. A model is about assumptions and validating those assumptions. You build models because it is too hard to build the real thing and throw it away if it does not work. You build models if you need to accelerate time and see what happens. You build models if you want to see all the places where a thing breaks.

You really need to determine if a prototype can be created using the same resources as a model. This is especially true if you are trying to surface qualitative measures and characteristics like functional requirements.

A TV Twilight Zone episode was about one of the greatest models ever created. It was a model of a planet like Earth, but in a lab setting in a small room next to the office of the scientist. Needless to say the episode ended with the scientist and his friend looking upon their model in horror as the inhabitants of their Earth annihilated each other in a horrific war. Their Earth was destroyed.

There was another model of the Earth created a few decades later in "The Hitch Hiker's Guide to the Galaxy". Interestingly Earth was created to address a previous model, which gave an answer of 42 after millions of years of run time. The Earth was supposed to clarify the original question from the original model.

Simulation modeling is what computer programs were about. In fact there was a category of staff computer programmers that existed and excelled in this area. Today everyone views computer programmers as application providers rather than great implementers of spectacular what-ifs in simulation and modeling activities. General modeling tools are only born from free flowing software simulations and models and can not be used in truly new state-of-the-art areas. Once an area of study matures there may be a possibility of codifying a tool so that other researchers and engineers can study a problem without needing a staff of brilliant simulation and modeling programmers.

There are a few different categories of models. They are:

1. Static Model: A static model is like an accounting ledger with entries. So you can use a spreadsheet to create a static model. It is a worst case analysis of a situation. It does not show behavior over time. You start with identifying your worst case scenario and translating it into a worst case set of inputs. You identify the key elements and what parameters they accept. These elements are then stimulated by your inputs. For example you can identify the amount of memory in a computer by identifying all the computer functions and their sizes. You can also identify the processing load by taking the functions, determining their processing path length, then multiplying them by the inputs.

2. Dynamic Model: A dynamic model is able to accept inputs over time. So it accepts your load scenario rather than a snapshot of the worst case set of inputs. The model internals are partitioned in the same way as a static model, but the behavior is modeled by using an algorithm representing the characteristics of the modeled elements and their interactions. For example your load scenario of an air traffic control algorithm might have airplanes fly crossing paths at various speeds to determine the probability of track swapping under various scenarios.

3. Simulation: A simulation is a dynamic model. It may use equipment similar to the actual thing being modeled, but not the actual thing because of prohibitive costs. In the worst case simulation it just might be software attempting to mimic the thing being modeled. In a better simulation it might be a cheaper version of the actual thing.

4. Emulation: Emulation uses the real thing to accept various inputs and determine behavior. This is the most faithful form of modeling, but it is extremely expensive and may not be able to support studies like accelerated time or beyond normal stress analysis.

Metrics

This is somewhat of a narrow topic, primarily related to software based systems. They seem to have the most difficulty with metrics.

All organizations gather metrics, even if they are not written down. We gather metrics to try to figure out what is going on, if there are problems, and to try to make things easier / better. Why do I start off this way, because many software organizations view metrics as an unnecessary burden taking away time from the "real work"? The "evil" metric data provides no insight into the real problems and can be misused within an organization. So the answer is to avoid metrics and just code the software. It's important to understand this because any metric data that is gathered needs to be "correct" and common across "different" activities so that meaningful comparisons can be performed. In the ideal situation the metrics should be gathered transparently, in the background, with little or no human intervention.

Cost and schedule are not good enough. More visibility is needed into an organization. Without this visibility the cost and schedule once blown is just that, blown. If finer grain data can be provided to show what may happen prior to losing the milestone, then corrective action can be taken sooner and less time and money might be wasted. A typical response is to develop plans with more milestones and shorter schedule cycles. This is called micro management and is usually a failure since it's not possible to anticipate activities and tasks below a certain level. So the answer is not to develop "better micro" schedules! The answer is to gather metrics and look at the data. All of the sudden management now needs to be engaged rather than just count the money.

The metrics data is trivial and useless for our real time systems so why do this? The software folks are busy trying to get basic functionality into the box and chasing real time problems. We need better real time tools and this paper stuff will not help us. These are the typical responses when the topic of software metrics surfaces.

So what does gathering information on the number of missing curly braces have to do with the serious problems in the lab? Some folks think that if these basic kinds of software quality characteristics are missing, then it's an indication of a stressed organization - an organization that is fighting with getting basic functionality into the box and getting it to work. The converse can be true where the team that goes out of its way to make "pretty code" has no emphasis on having the box perform. However, if that approach is taken, testing and the metrics associated with testing should surface that "bad" approach. So it's a balance. Don't go out of the way to stress that the code "be pretty" at the expense of working functionality. If this balance between the "software" and "test" metrics is maintained, then there is a reasonable set of software metrics. Remember that the test metrics counter balance the software metrics.

What data should we collect - tricky question. The problem is to minimize the noise so that the real information can be detected from the data. However, in one instance data considered noise becomes valuable information in another instance. So visualization is key to being able to reduce the noise level. What should be gathered - anything that is easy to count on a consistent basis.

Who should look at these things - everyone. They should be used to help understand where there are potential issues. The metrics should also percolate to the organizational level. The organizational level should use this information to gain a better insight into how things are progressing, given that cost and schedule indicators are usually too late, they are just a confirmation of a problem.

Although the previous metrics discussion was centered on software, metrics are important everywhere. As you consider the sustainable development problem, consider this simple metrics discussion. It has invaluable lessons that should never be avoided. Some of the more visible lessons are:

- You must gather metrics
- You don't know what to capture so capture everything
- Do the capture transparently
- There is too much lag in money metrics
- Relying only on money & schedule will result in failure
- Real metrics data force people to understand their business
- Visualization tools are imperative
- Everyone should have access to the metrics

Key Requirements and Issues

Identifying and tracking the key requirements and issues may mean the difference between success and failure. Not all requirements and issues are the same. Some are make or break situations. Key requirements are drivers of the system solutions. They can be technology, performance, cost, schedule, production, maintenance, logistics, support, and other drivers. These drivers may exist because the state of the art is being pushed in an area or previous knowledge shows these requirements and issues are make or break items.

Everyone should know the key requirements. They should never be hidden. It is possible that some requirements and issues are so significant that management will try to hide them, but then no one will be able to use the magic of their abilities to tackle and address these key requirements. In the end the key requirements and issues don't go away, they always remain, but the successful team has addressed and effectively satisfied each of the key requirements and knows how the key issues were closed. It is the essence of the solution.

Key requirements and issues come in layers. There are key requirements and issues at the highest level and are parts of the architecture dialog. There are key requirements and issues at the subsystem levels. There are key requirements and issues at the component levels. There are key requirements and issues at the abstract levels like maintenance, training, support, and other areas that do not make up the physical solution but are part of the system solution.

So key requirements and issues are very important. In many ways they are the kickoff of the activity. Everyone tries to find them then everyone wraps around them until they are one with the key requirements and issues. Yes it is like "Zen and the Art of Motorcycle Maintenance".

Study The Past

The other day I was curious about system engineering references on Wikipedia. I arrived directly on a page dedicated to system engineering. That page had various references to operations research and other related topics. Curiously I eventually arrived at a discussion of how the very first computer music was created in Australia. I was shocked and surprised to see that Australia had their very first computer about the same time as the United States. Apparently they created the very first computer generated music.

The computer music link eventually took my research into guitar amplifiers and large venue concert sound systems. That eventually took me into amplifiers. As I started to read the amplifier discussion I learned that there were other amplifiers other than electrical sound amplification. I ran into a reference of mechanical amplifiers, which took me to the differential analyzer from Vannevar Bush.

I clicked into the link for Dr. Vannevar Bush and something incredible happened. I learned about the memex conceived by Vannevar in 1945. I then accessed "Science The Endless Frontier, A Report to the President by Dr. Vannevar Bush, Director of the Office of Scientific Research and Development, July 1945" that was provided to President Roosevelt. I then clicked into the National Science Foundation (NSF), which was proposed in this incredible paper presented to President Roosevelt. From there I saw the funding provided by the NSF which gave birth to packet switched networks and to the Mosaic processor. I realized at that moment that the NSF was implementing the Vannevar dream first proposed in 1945. This paper is so important I have included it in this book as an appendix. Please go there and read this paper if you read nothing else in this book. To see my research trails here are the key links:

- http://en.wikipedia.org/wiki/Memex
- http://www.nsf.gov/about/history/vbush1945.htm
- http://en.wikipedia.org/wiki/National_Science_Foundation

The most incredible part of this simple work is that I started a simple research project without realizing it. I used Vannevars' machine to actually perform the research and learn not only where the Internet really started but also where my personal technology and science values originated. The Vannevar letter to President Roosevelt set the policy for an entire generation, my generation.

After the enormous joy of finally learning the origins of the Internet and where my science and engineering values were defined, I eventually had a horrific realization. Vannevar Bush died in 1974. He never saw the Internet. Vannevar Bush was probably part of an entire generation of thinkers that set our values after WWII. Those values allowed us to uplift humanity and move it in a positive direction like at no other time in history. Sadly as that generation passed away new values have been put in place, in many cases the values that existed before the great wars. Self-interest and the markets are viewed as the mechanism to solve all problems. History teaches otherwise and great men and women in the last century took strong steps to not repeat the mistakes of history. At this moment there is only an echo of this work in people like me. We were never formally introduced into the work of people like Vannevar Bush, except in extreme isolated cases. There is another generation beyond mine that does not even have a faint echo of these great thoughts and works. This is a problem.

Connections

In many ways the previous discussion was a discussion of connections. Science and engineering are based on connections. You need to do a literature search before you propose new science. You need to understand current solutions before you can propose a new engineering approach. This is what the memex was about, this is what the Internet can be, the research tool to tie 5000 plus years of civilization together.

Now for the dream, with 6 billion well fed educated people able to live to their maximum desired potential, anything is possible. This would be less of a problem if people could live for 1000 years or 10,000 years but they don't and so humans need the library. The library connects and binds all the work of all the generations. It remains to be seen what will be done with the memex.

So what does this mean for you in your project or program? Research for the sake of research is good. You have an obligation to maintain a library and allow free flow of information. If you don't do this then you are engaged in a deviant self-serving practice that betrays the work of all the Vannevar Bushs throughout time.

There is a time for secrets. Vannevar Bush of all people understood that time. There is also a time of sharing. Vannevar Bush also understood that time. The memex is not a machine of secrets. It is not a machine that takes a coin to access a conference proceeding. The memex is survival of humanity. Go ahead and look at these connections:

- http://en.wikipedia.org/wiki/System_engineering
- http://en.wikipedia.org/wiki/CSIRAC (tubes)
- http://en.wikipedia.org/wiki/Voice_of_the_customer (end)
- http://en.wikipedia.org/wiki/2n3055 (end)
- http://en.wikipedia.org/wiki/Instrument_amplifier
- http://en.wikipedia.org/wiki/RCA (end)
- http://en.wikipedia.org/wiki/Amplifier (mechanical amp)
- http://en.wikipedia.org/wiki/Vannevar_Bush
- http://en.wikipedia.org/wiki/Differential_analyzer (end)
- http://en.wikipedia.org/wiki/Autopilot (end)
- http://en.wikipedia.org/wiki/Memex
- http://en.wikipedia.org/wiki/United_States_National_Research_Council
- http://en.wikipedia.org/wiki/National_Defense_Research_Committee
- http://en.wikipedia.org/wiki/Office_of_Scientific_Research_and_Development
- http://www.nsf.gov/about/history/vbush1945.htm
- http://en.wikipedia.org/wiki/National_Science_Foundation
- http://en.wikipedia.org/wiki/Internet
- http://en.wikipedia.org/wiki/National_Center_for_Supercomputing_Applications
- http://en.wikipedia.org/wiki/Mosaic_%28web_browser%29
- http://www.nsf.gov/news/special_reports/cyber/digitallibraries.jsp
- http://en.wikipedia.org/wiki/Google
- http://en.wikipedia.org/wiki/High_Performance_Computing_and_Communication_Act_of_1991

There is a wonderful TV series from 1978 called "Connections". It tracks 12,000 years of science history in a ten part series that took 14 months to film. The series covers 19 countries and 150 locations. This is what we do as humans. We build upon the work of others.

Research

You are either growing or you are rotting. That was a statement made by someone in the real estate business giving a class on New Jersey real estate licensure in 1978.

Every engineering organization needs to eventually answer the question: are we production, development, or research. Most choose production and or development. That means they are rotting. They are dead organizations with no future. All potential is sapped out. These are dark dreary organizations filled with really self-serving stupid people.

Research is what makes the world go around. It does not matter if you flip hamburgers for a living or you are system engineering a sustainable development wonder. Everyone eventually gets a new idea no matter what they do and that idea needs to be tried and refined. Those that claim they make money and don't do research need to be left in the middle of a desert with a bottle of water, a box of Twinkies, and then told to strip those assets as the vehicles speed away into the desert sun. Let's see if they come back and part the sea.

Ok so lets look at some R&D numbers from 2006:
- $343 US billion United States 2.6% of GDP
- $231 US billion EU 1.8% of GDP
- $130 US billion Japan 3.2 % of GDP
- $115 US billion China

R&D as a percent of revenues in 2006:
- 3.5% industrial company
- 7.0% computer manufacturer
- 15% high technology company
- 25% Ericsson (engineering company)
- 43% Allergan (a biotech company)

However the story is not in the numbers. I will claim that progress has stalled and we are only reaping the benefits of miniaturization started in the last century. It has been over 30 years since the first energy crisis in the USA and essentially nothing has happened. I will make the claim, that like in "Gullivers Travels" we have become Laputians, studying the useless and searching for the next hot product regardless if it is needed or even if it works. Meanwhile the world is getting more complex needing the attention of some serious solutions that can only come from some serious fundamental and applied research.

Research became an ugly word in the journey towards productivity at the tail end of the last century. It was a reaction to the 1970s threats that seemed to surface from no where. The reality is these threats did not come from a dark hole, they were natural as the world finally started to dig itself out of the WWII fiasco. The problem is the USA panicked and in the process the USA lost research centers that we will never be able to recreate. We even lost the thought process of research as all funds were diverted towards incremental product development. It became ingrained when downsizing kicked in and people changed their thought processes within all institutions.

It was terrifying for me to see companies throw away thinkers and dreamers. These were people who were once respected and revered for their very special abilities. It was even harder for me to see R&D budgets diverted towards failing programs or to offset the cost of proposed programs. The final horror was to see the systematic closing of physical libraries in these organizations in the name of cost cutting.

Productivity

Productivity and research go together. You can not have one without the other. I will state however that research comes first. Many people confuse efficient work with productivity but if the work does not produce value then there is no output. Conversely the output can be very valuable but come at great cost because of inefficiency. Determining the output from an effort may take a long time. For example efforts that produce short-term gain may devastate the long-term result and outstanding long-term results may require the sacrifice of short-term possibilities. This was reduced by the WWII generation to the statement of "pay me now or pay me more later".

In the last decade and a half of the last century this was misapplied to individuals. It was not uncommon to find stupid management driven by self-interest invalidate the work of people that would have great value. They would autocratically arrive and just state the work had no value and terminate the effort, group, or department. This left millions of high tech workers confused and many times without a job. With the next go round in the job sequence these workers made sure they checked their minds, creativity, innovation, initiative and egos at the parking lots of their new prisons and just followed the orders of the inmates that were now in control.

Yes I used very caustic words. These are the words spoken by the people in these settings. These words are fact. Some folks are lucky these are just words. In previous generations such behavior resulted in massive social unrest as money was funneled into unknown areas and whole areas of growth and opportunity were destroyed.

Process

Process is not static. It is like a living thing changing and evolving as other things in the process setting change. Organizations change because they also display the attributes of a living thing, continually changing and evolving with the seasons of our times to paraphrase a wonderful Rock Group from the last century, Renaissance, in one of their works "A Song for All Seasons". Beautiful stuff, just like a living process and organization.

Look here is the deal, if you are creating a solution to a problem you need to identify how you will "build" that solution. What information products will you produce, how will they tie together, what tools and techniques will you use or create, and what the issues are in building the beast. It does not matter if it is a re-spin of something that has existed for 100 years or if you are building your very first starship with warp drive.

Day one identify how you think you will tackle the job, write it down, start doing it, if it does not work or has problems, modify it, then change the written description of the process. The trick is to not do this in isolation. Every stakeholder needs to own the process. They have to agree to the process, love the process, and make it work. It is not the job of management to force a process on those that will implement the process. However management is an equal stakeholder in the process. The best way to make management a stakeholder in the process is to give them technical tasks that feed the process.

Here are the fundamentals of assessing your organization. You are either very mature, somewhat mature, a babe in the woods, or stupid. You know where you fit and now is a good time to introduce:

"On Bullshit" from Princeton professor Harry G. Frankfurt, Winner of the 2005 Bestseller Awards, Philosophy Category:

http://www.pupress.princeton.edu/titles/7929.html

The levels of consciousness are:

1. Chaos everything is random you don't know what anyone will do next, things are very political, lots of liars and bullshit artists, and honest folks are afraid, management prays on the innocent
2. Things tend to get done in a repeatable way, everyone knows what everyone else is doing and how their part fits into the collective
3. You have documented processes that people follow and the documents are maintained, in other words they always represent more or less what is happening no matter the time of the year or what year it happens to be
4. You actually start to measure stuff that matters, everyone knows those measures and are not afraid of the measures because everyone is enlightened enough to not fry anyone in the group, so it's not about shallow productivity asset stripping schemes by corrupt management
5. Based on your metrics you evaluate new techniques, technologies, tools and you are able to make qualitative and quantitative predictions about their introduction into the process

So these basic principles apply to all organizations and all time frames. They are not hundreds of pages, they do not take special training, and they do not use armies of strangers looking at your proprietary process, the billion-dollar process that separates you from everyone else in the world.

Let's repeat the first part of this diatribe: day one, identify how you think you will tackle the job. So lets assume you are in pre proposal phase or you are conceptualizing a new product. When your technical staff prepares their technical presentation, have them identify how they think the job will be tackled. If they can't identify how the job will be done to build this new thing they are proposing then maybe the solution is not viable. So the two are tied together - the technical solution and can it be built using either current approaches or a new equally break through approach.

The reality is that breakthrough solutions also require break through processes. Just so I am clear: methods, processes, tools, techniques. It's not about Gantt charts from project management worlds.

Now here is an important little secret about process. If you document a process that works and is proven over years of operation you can not move it wholesale to a new organization. That process is bound to that organization. The reality is if an organization has anything of value its people transition from apprentice to journeymen to master over the span of years. It takes anywhere from 2-5 years to transition from apprentice to journeymen. So no matter how detailed the process description, everyone new to the process is an apprentice regardless of experience in other organizations. Again, that is if the organization has anything of real value to offer - for example top three in an industry where there are many players.

That is why when organizations document their processes then attempt to replace staff they self-destruct.

So why should you take the time to document your processes? It is about bringing in new apprentice staff and getting them on board as fast as possible and it is about visualizing the operation so that continual improvement can follow new technologies, products, and techniques.

Publishing

One day I did an Internet search of "Office of System Engineering Management". There were 6 links, 4 were books and 2 were studies from Lincoln Labs and MITRE. The Internet search engine results were:

*1. **Technical Development Plan for a Discrete Address Beacon System**. The document presents a technical development plan for such a system; this plan was developed within the Office of System Engineering Management and the*
stinet.dtic.mil/oai/oai?verb=getRecord&metadataPrefix=html&id entifier=AD0732585 - 4k -

*2. **Preliminary Computer Sizing Estimates for Automated En Route ATC** As an early input to the requirements analysis effort, the FAA's Office of System Engineering Management requested a preliminary analysis of computer loads*
stinet.dtic.mil/oai/oai?verb=getRecord&metadataPrefix=html&id entifier=ADA082628 - 6k

A Federally Funded Research and Development Center, MITRE, produced one document and a University Lab, MIT Lincoln Labs, produced the other document. This was paid for by the taxpayer in the 1970's. In the past, before the Internet the Government Printing Office was chartered with distributing documents to the public for a nominal fee of 5 cents per page with a very steep discount as the page count went up. Rarely would a document exceed $5 dollars. Most of the time the documents were available from the originating organization or the Government for free as one of the job functions of serving the people of the USA.

Clicking into these links takes me to one of several organizations. To make a long story short the price of the 18 page document was $45 dollars. It has a new number assigned by some third party organization. Its original number issued by the FAA was FAA-EM-79-21. This other organization boasts how they have a database of millions of documents, which sets their value at billions of dollars.

Now when were the assets of the people converted to a money machine? The constitution and a few hundred years of precedent guarantee intellectual property in the Unites States and intellectual property is always owned by a person and assigned to an entity, like a company or the Government. The people who worked in companies and other organizations willingly offered their intellectual property to the United States but not to this organization, especially for the purpose of making money. This is plain old theft of intellectual property on a grand scale.

A number of years ago I published several papers at low level conferences. I was led to believe that this was in the interest of the free flow of science and engineering. The papers assigning my Intellectual property were to the conference and its proceedings. This was in the interest of not having multiple conferences present the same paper. When the Internet arrived I posted my papers on my web site, years later. Systematically I was contacted by each organization and in a very threatening voice directed to remove my intellectual property from my web site.

I stopped publishing even though I have been requested and invited many times to express my ideas. That is why you are reading this book on this media. No one will ever steal anything from me again - it's over and I suspect there are millions of people engaged in high tech who feel the same way with their own unique stories. Back on track, publishing has become a very serious issue - it is seriously broken.

In the old days companies and other organizations maintained vast libraries with access to all conference material in their industries and areas of work. Those libraries have been removed so typical staff has no access to conference proceedings from professional societies. These conferences have become very closed communities with no one of any value gaining the benefit of this shared social industry work.

Technical societies in their infinite wisdom have restricted web access to the papers even though many authors produced works long before the Internet in a time and place where their work was always available from their institutions at the physical library. So many authors have stopped participating, including this author.

Executives love this because they feel they protect proprietary work. Forget about having someone screening papers for technical conferences, that position no longer exists in many organizations. No one from the company or country is leaking information. It's a wonderful turn of events.

The problem with this state of affairs is that high technology as we knew and loved it after WWII is shutting down. There is further evidence of this shutdown if you examine the number of Research and Development labs that have been eliminated in the United States.

However if you wish to publish and you are member of a technical society and you need some criteria for screening papers, here is what each of you should follow:

1. What is the problem you are trying to address?
2. What are the current approaches to addressing the problem?
3. What is wrong with the current approaches?
4. What are the potential solutions to the problem (optional)?
5. What is the proposed solution to the problem?
6. Why is the proposed solution to the problem the best solution?

It is truly amazing, but even technical societies have lost these simple rules when reviewing potential publications. This is a serious issue and must be solved if we are to start to address the huge challenges in this next century.

Creativity and Innovation

There is a simple formula that can be applied by anyone to spur creativity and innovation. The issue is can the practitioners practice this simple formula. Do they have the freedom and liberty to engage in this simple yet incredibly powerful technique? The formula is Saturate, Incubate, Synthesize, Optimize, and Select.

1. <u>Saturate</u> is exactly as the word implies. Immerse yourself in the material, no matter how mundane or irrelevant it may seem in the beginning. Talk to everyone about the material and dialog if possible.
2. <u>Incubate</u> is exactly as the word implies. Sleep on it and let the miracle of the human mind go to work on the problem.
3. <u>Synthesis</u> happens after incubation. You can't stop it; it is human. Eventually approaches will start to surface. Mature these approaches as you continue to saturate and incubate.
4. <u>Optimize</u> is as the word implies, take each viable approach and move it to its most elegant limit.
5. <u>Select</u> you guessed it, pick your best approach.

This process of creativity dovetails in and out of the system engineering process that unfolds in this document. It is hard to say if they are separate or one and the same, but I like to think I practice both at the same time.

Program Project or Project Program

So which is it? Projects make up programs, period. So programs are bigger than projects. Programs are successful by definition because it takes more than one project to make a program. Programs are like product lines but programs may be made of multiple products and product lines.

It is critical that a valid charter be established for the project or program. The charter needs to be a succinct statement of why the project or program exists and what it is to accomplish. Everyone should be aware of the charter. Day one on the job, as part of briefing the program or project, the charter must be clearly stated to the new members.

Never start a project unless the financial box is big enough to support the charter and initial goals. If no one is willing to commit reasonable funds to tackle the problem, don't waste the money. Apply the money to an existing project or wait until proper funding with a reasonable schedule can be established. If funds are never made available for reasonable projects then let the organization self-destruct in its own greed. Move to another organization and make sure you tell everyone your story.

Do not confuse these words with individual, grass roots, or mom and pop business operations. These worlds use completely different criteria when deciding to start a project. Usually there is no funding and all work is based on sweat equity.

The problem is when large institutions, governments, and corporations ignore economies of scale and run parallel operations modeled after individual, grass roots, or mom and pop organizations. These Darwinian entities waste enormous resources even though they may show short-term gains to investors. In a twist of language reminiscent of "1984" these organizations advertise themselves as ecological organizations not realizing it is about symbiosis.

Where Do Requirements Come From

Requirements come from the cabbage patch. Ok, so here is the real story. Be prepared, it will be painful. It depends on the type of program.

If you are in the middle of a program that is yet another spin of an established industry, product, or product line, then the requirements exist and they come from the organization. Typically the requirements are part of the culture and locked in people's heads. If the organization is mature, then there are libraries containing information products such as previous studies and specifications. If the outfit is a really mature organization you might actually have your requirements in a System Requirements Database (SRDB) repository. So, all you are really doing is duplicating what has been done in the past with a slight spin and perhaps a new element which requires a few new requirements. Creating these new requirements in this established organization now becomes tricky because you may need to follow some of the principles of requirements development that are used for new "clean slate" programs. So, keep reading.

If you are on a new program with a clean slate, then the requirements generation process is a sight to behold, if it's done "properly". There is a picture. You have to visualize it. Draw it on a napkin if needed as you read the next few sentences. The input shows personal inputs, brainstorm sessions, round table discussions. However, this does not do justice to the process that is actually used to create requirements from nothing for your clean slate program. What really happens is affectionately called studies and there are large numbers of studies and participants. The reason for the large number is to gain all the perspectives before the implementation machine is activated. For example, you might have a group of people examining a half dozen implementations of existing similar systems. There might be a group of people performing architecture tradeoff studies allocating equipment within buildings across the planet and its orbit. There might be a group of people studying different algorithms for accomplishing a very narrow task like tracking commercial aircraft in various stages of flight. There might be people creating fault trees looking for single points of failure that need to be removed from the system. People might even be creating prototypes of various aspects of the future system. There could be simulations using existing infrastructure of machines and people. The participants can range from subject matter experts who were or are operational personnel on similar systems to a lone Ph.D. implementing a thesis as a new technology is being developed. These studies no matter how small or how grand result in requirements.

The requirements need to be made consistent, complete, and testable. They also need to be organized into groups that represent similar in kind (functional and temporal cohesion) and similar in level (system, segment, subsystem, or configuration item like hardware or software). The requirements are captured in specifications. Requirements are never held within analysis / study information products. They always must be transferred to the specification tree.

Why the emphasis on organization of the requirements? It's driven by the fact that we are humans and that we can only handle about 6 things at any given instant, unless we are weird. It's also driven by a process, which tries to identify missing requirements. This process is known as traceability and the goal is to see that all parent and child requirements have links. For example, a software designer might surface a requirement from that perspective which was never seen from other related perspectives. That means a high level requirement might be missing that this lone designer surfaced as a result of that painful detail. That high level requirement might now impact a dozen other designers that need a similar detailed requirement in their part of the machine. The same thing can happen at a higher level, where a subject matter expert (SME) walks in, reviews the system, and starts to laugh. The laughter may be the result of a fundamental principal that exists in other similar systems that surely will exist in this system. That one principal might translate to one high level requirement which might translate into hundreds of lower level requirements.

The purpose of traceability is to support the great hunt for missing and conflicting requirements. So, requirements do come from the cabbage patch! Keep reading :)

System Requirements Databases

The previous discussion on the hunt for requirements is a lead into this topic. Why do I need a System Requirements Database (SRDB) using a thing like DOORS?

DOORS is a product from a company called QSS which sold off to Telelogic which sold off to IBM which was preceded by RDD which was preceded by custom software on mainframe computers at special companies like Hughes Aircraft.

The story begins over 30 years ago, circa 1977 - 1980. At the time people were excited about a process called structured system analysis and structured programming. The process acknowledged that people could only relate to about 6 things at any given moment. So the idea was to create a process that did just that, captured a system view at a particular level, which did not exceed 6 things, well ok, maybe 15 or 20. That view would then be exploded with another view that would contain about 6 things. The decomposition would continue until the analysts could go no further, they would reach the leaves of a wondrous tree. At the same time people were claiming that most project failures could be traced to bad requirements. They were missing, incomplete, inconsistent, vague, conflicting, and a bunch of other bad stuff. Additionally, even though computers were an expensive piece of infrastructure at the time, there were people also starting to think of new computer based tools to organize information and the relational database was a topic of discussion.

So, you have these three elements flowing around in the community: structured analysis, bad requirements, and relational databases. Like all great moments in history, someone made a connection and the idea was born to place requirements into a relational database. Those requirements could then be grouped (allocated to functions), leveled (placed into the system, segment, subsystem, or component levels), and links could be created to look for those missing requirements. What a great idea! It was a sight to behold in a major aerospace company with mainframe resources and folks building a new SRDB tool from the ground up and populating it, all for the sole purpose of creating a new system. Talk about challenges.

Other people may have other stories of where this stuff came from, but that story is probably as good as the others.

Fast forward 20 plus years. Looks like the idea was ok. There is now a commercial infrastructure with companies offering SRDB tools. The part that is missing is the process that uses the SRDB tool. But we know what to do:

1. We do studies for the sole purpose of surfacing requirements
2. We organize those requirements into functional areas and levels
3. We capture those requirements in an SRDB tool (one fancy hairy relational database)
4. We create parent child reports and look for missing, incomplete, inconsistent, vague, conflicting, un-testable requirements using the SRDB and clever mining tools that crunch the SRDB reports.

Requirements Goals and Dreams

Goals are tomorrow's requirements. Dreams are next week's requirements. When we stop making goals and loose our dreams we stop progress. The challenge is to constantly challenge ourselves and every so often greatness happens when least expected. So always keep track of your Requirements, Goals, and Dreams. You now have the technology. Write specifications to house your requirements and figure out how to make your dreams come true.

What Ifs

Some of us have practiced thought experiments. This is where you post a problem in your head and take it to its natural logical conclusions. Some of us have created scenarios. Like the thought experiment except scenarios are written down and rather than being very private they are a group activity where others influence the problem. Prototypes are yet another way to study a problem and see what should be done before large-scale roll out of a solution is provided. So what is the "what if"?

The "what if" is practiced almost every day by everyone. When someone sits down to write a memo or email, the first draft is a "what if". The first spin of a spreadsheet is a "what if".

The problem is people ignore this simple everyday experience once it comes to process. Every process, method, technique, tool button pressing, tool report must be vetted with "what if" sequences. This is one of the primary failures of new tool introductions and process formalization in immature people and organizations.

Questions or Answers

So it's not about the answers. It is about the questions. The second ultimate computer in the universe, Deep Thought, from "The Hitch Hikers Guide to the Galaxy", bought home that point with in your face clarity. The WWII generation always tried to tell their kids it's about the questions and not the answers, but we rarely listened. As the WWII generation passed, fewer and fewer people were asking questions. That mode of operation was purged from company halls and you were labeled as someone who could not close if you asked questions. That was essentially a career showstopper. This happened in the span of 5 years. Prior to that some organizations encouraged you to ask questions and tied it to your ability to engage in the process.

The problem is the answers are irrelevant. It is always all about the questions. In fact if the right questions are asked then the answers fall out, they become self-evident. The problem here is that in an environment of "question suppression" bullshit artists and liar's frame questions such that their agenda can succeed. This was finally surfaced in the famous small book from a Princeton professor, "On Bullshit".

So the answer is not 42. It is the pursuit of your ultimate question and then the question that matters. I will never forget the bums in one corporation funded 100% by the US taxpayer I had the misfortune to be part of. They would state we don't want you to ask questions. We want you to do, now go to work and do. This entity had zero investment in anything and would buy what they needed via hiring people previously trained and filled with intellectual property from other entities then fire them in pursuit of the next strip mining exercise. This was outright theft.

System Safety and Certification

We are all engineers, mathematicians, scientists, and artists. Most of us fear system safety and certification and yet we all rely on this basic concept. Even engineers who do not work in civil engineering and never go through the process of getting a professional engineer's license fear this. Engineers are exposed to this in their formal education but they tend to ignore it as courses with little relevance. Yet we all rely on certified and safe systems. Everyday we wake up in houses that do not collapse, we use water that does not sicken our children, we travel in cars on roads that rarely kill us, and we fly in airplanes that do not fall from the sky.

In the past most engineering and scientific organizations did not have to deal with system safety and certification, so the engineer's mathematician's scientists and artists did not focus in this area. Things are now changing, as technology is able to seep into more aspects of our infrastructure.

The problem is our formal education usually gives us examples that are very poor from a system safety and certification point of view. For example, software students study languages, information structures, patterns, techniques of handling information, and language syntax. They all get very excited about syntax. It becomes a race for the most abstract syntax that is the cleverest use of a language. The problem is that this syntax is usually unsafe and as such causes people responsible with certification responsibility to rail against a solution that no one wants to go back and change.

What are the elements of system safety? It begins with architecture and ends with implementation details.

Safe architectures are resilient and fault tolerant. Some applications like Air Traffic Control or bridges are extremely complex and challenging where the basic services need to be provided no matter what the system encounters and how its elements fail. Other applications like a nuclear power facility are challenging but are permitted to shut down in the presence of failure.

There are different techniques that are applied to safe architectures. One technique is to apply fault tolerance where elements are duplicated and the outputs are checked or work together. This is essentially duplicating something once twice or however many times needed to achieve the desired level of fault tolerance. An example of this is 4 computers that vote on the output or a bridge that uses 10,000 support elements that span various points of the structure. Another technique is to use orthogonal mechanisms that check each other in a symbiotic solution. An example of this would be a progress counter in a computer or the use of ferries in addition to a bridge to cross a waterway.

There are different techniques that are used or avoided during implementation. In the case of software most programmers use a syntax of decision called the non explicit if statement. Its structure is the simple *if (parameter)*. The problem is that the decision is true for all values greater than one, however the check is usually applied for checking only 1 value. The other values though not possible in the logic of the program can surface in the presence of a failure, like an alpha particle flipping the bit of a memory location. Another egregious unsafe software technique is the use of *ifdef* compile switches. People born on the PC platform are notorious users of this extremely dangerous approach. The problem is that the ifdef can be set improperly at build time, building the wrong thing and that thing can make it out into the field. The software may work, but it may be a lab version of the software, which contains paths never tested. In an operational setting those paths could cost someone their life. This simple structure also makes the software much more difficult to analyze and determine if all valid paths have been tested. Each domain has their gremlins and they all need to be understood and properly addressed.

System safety needs to include architectural and implementation elements. Unfortunately the implementation elements become very specialized and unique to the domain. So the trick is to surface these elements and have everyone come up to speed on why these elements are needed and how they work. The problem arises when secrecy surfaces as entities try to protect what they feel is intellectual property or other interests. You have a choice, either use the full transparency principles outlined in this book or risk killing people in the name of a few short term dollars. The reality is many of these techniques become self evident to practitioners. So those engaged in the area have little excuse for keeping them hidden. What is important is to make sure all techniques have been identified, vetted, then applied using sound engineering and scientific principles.

Vision And Architecture

Each approach in a tradeoff needs to have an advocate. That advocate needs to maintain the ideal vision of that approach or architecture. It is like an operational amplifier in a hardware circuit analysis. An OP AMP has infinite gain and bandwidth, yet no such device exits. The ideal architecture or approach then degrades as the science and engineering is applied to the trade studies. At some point the ideal vision may no longer be possible and the approach may actually exhibit a catastrophic failure.

Examples of elements that degrade the ideal vision are Technology, Politics, Money, Time, Motivation, Education, and People. The only valid reason for an architecture vision to degrade should be technology. Everything else is fixable.

It's All Relative

I came to this all-important observation as I approached my 4th decade on earth. I was never shown this nor was it ever discussed.

You always view yourself as the youngest year you can remember, typically as a baby, and you view others the first day you meet them. So your older brother or sister is always older and more mature even though you yourself may be 50. When you are 50 and you meet someone for the first time that is 55 you will always view them as 55, you will never see them as being younger. This actually sets expectations in your own head that may be unreasonable.

So on the first day of high school everything having to do with high school is new, it is 99% new. By the start of your fourth year of high school only 25% should be new. However, the most important stuff, the top 10% is learned the first year. But this frame of reference is that of a high school student. There are other frames of reference and they mature in the same way. This is an example of frames of reference most can relate to: baby, child, kid, teen, college, young adult, adult, parent, empty nester, retired. Placed on a scale:

Yr	Phase	Baby	Child	Kid	Teen
1	baby	33	100	100	100
2	baby	66	100	100	100
3	baby	100	100	100	100
4	child	0	50	100	100
5	child	0	100	100	100
6	kid	0	0	14	100
7	kid	0	0	28	100
8	kid	0	0	42	100
9	kid	0	0	56	100
10	kid	0	0	70	100
11	kid	0	0	84	100
12	kid	0	0	100	100
13	teen	0	0	0	17
14	teen	0	0	0	34
15	teen	0	0	0	51
16	teen	0	0	0	68
17	teen	0	0	0	85
18	teen	0	0	0	100

So just when you master becoming a baby you are pushed into the child frame of reference. Just when you master being a child you are pushed into the kid frame of reference. Babies know nothing about being a child. A child knows nothing about being a kid, and so on through each phase, its maturity curve and transition to the next phase.

This surfaced when attempting to properly raise my own children. It was a simple way to communicate that they are engaging in areas well outside their area of understanding.

This same relationship holds true in every aspect of System Engineering and Management.

Methods and Frameworks

At this point you are probably wondering where are the other traditional system engineering techniques. Where is the discussion on topics like:

1. Functional Flow Diagrams
2. Operational Sequence Diagrams
3. Functional Block Diagrams

4. IDEF (ICAM Definition Languages)
5. ICAM (Integrated Computer-Aided Manufacturing)
6. DODAF (Department of Defense Architecture Framework)
7. SysML (Systems Modeling Language)
8. Structured System Analysis
9. Data Flow Diagrams
10. Interface Diagrams
11. Hierarchical Input Processing Output (HIPO) Diagrams
12. Flow Charts
13. Decomposition Trees
14. N-Squared Analysis
15. Control Theory

And the list goes on and on.

They are not discussed because they are available in the general body of knowledge. Some of the items on that list are based on set theory and logic. For example, many people can eventually relate to a flow chart and a functional block diagram. However, I will say something very important relative to the formal and semi formal methods listed.

As soon as you introduce a technique that is not based on words and a simple picture, you start to lose 98% of your stakeholders. The only people who can relate to the formal methods are those trained in the formal method and who use the formal method on a daily basis. It does not mean you can't use it to try to understand the problem from a different perspective. It just means that it becomes a detailed study that needs to be summarized with words and a picture that everyone understands.

Further, you can not use one or more of these formal methods to replace what is discussed in this book. On the one hand this book represents a framework, but unlike frameworks it clearly makes the point that you push beyond any known patterns, including all known frameworks. Otherwise you are not pushing to the next level that is unique to your charter.

You are also probably wondering about frameworks and some traditional elements like:

1. Operational Concept
2. Requirements Analysis
3. Functional Analysis
4. Performance Analysis
5. Synthesis
6. Design
7. Implementation
8. Test
9. Validation
10. Maintenance
11. Decommissioning

Again, these items are not discussed because they are available in the general body of knowledge. What are not available in the general body of knowledge are the items highlighted in this book. In some ways these items are a guide to help execute these methods and frameworks. They come from the journey of apprentice to journeymen, to mentor. In many ways they may be all you need, depending on your role, to participate as an active stakeholder in the process.

Finally, this is very important, you draw on 5000 years of civilization, not some narrow framework that someone calls system engineering. The only thing that matters in system engineering is that there is a search for truth and the MOE is a way to help surface that truth. So today it is N-Squared analysis. Tomorrow it might be a new analysis technique invented by someone with a major new insight while trying to solve a problem not solvable with any known techniques.

I need to offer a word of caution about the MOE. Do not confuse this with cost benefit analysis. Cost benefit analysis is usually practiced by management while trying to stack the deck in favor of a particular solution. History contains many examples of failures by those who practiced this technique. The MOE is based on full transparency and the inclusion of all stakeholders. This essentially forces the full set of criteria to be considered using all the available techniques of science and art from 5000 years of civilization.

Bachelor of Arts

Occasionally system engineers come from the arts like Philosophy or History. At the university level they are introduced to the great works of our civilizations. When they leave the university they then get exposed to the current state of affairs. This is a list of some of the more important aspects of the arts in engineering.

Many people without a formal education in the arts can relate to and understand these items but they fail to follow through on the right direction to take. This is a list of the engineering arts with brief descriptions, comments, lessons, and warnings that can be used as guidance so that things do not become difficult, impossible, or useless and so that people not only survive but thrive and grow in the setting.

Performance and Management Failure

All failures are management failures. At no time should responsibility of failure be pushed down. With authority comes responsibility. Empowerment should be pushed down to the lowest levels not blame. There should never be scapegoats.

We all vibrate to different colors of light. Everyone has a special area where they shine. Put us together and there is a spectacular glow. The trick is to find that color and match it to what needs to be done in the organization. That is very different from, I have this thing that needs to be done this way now go do it or you have no value. High tech organizations engaged in meaningful activity can always find a place for any color of light. When these organizations have problems, the term skills mix surfaces. The problem is not skill mix but the organization, which can not consume the output of its creative, innovative, inventive and thus productive members. The organization is sick because the management has failed.

Critical Thinking and Gulliver's Travels

There is a wonderful TV miniseries version of this fairy tail, "Gulliver's Travels", created in 1996. Pettiness, paranoia, delusions of grandeur, pomposity, and superciliousness are some of the topics.

In one scene Gulliver visits the land of Laputians a place where there is a great seat of learning where some people study mathematics, astronomy, music and technology. As he enters this great seat of learning he is shocked to see that all the professors are studying useless things. In many ways they are all insane.

It is about critical thinking and being able to punch through the irrelevant. Who cares about how many angels can dance on the head of a pin? Being inundated with information is a sure sign that something is wrong. The danger here is that someone filters the information in an effort to steer critical thinking results. So this is a delicate balance.

Management and Its Role

Many modern management classes begin with the following classic exchange from "The Memorabilia" by Xenophon:

--- **Socrates**. *Seeing Nicomachides on his way back from the magistrate elections, asked: Who are elected generals, Nicomachides?*

Nicomachides. *Will these Athenians never change, Socrates? To go and elect, not me, who has literally worn myself out with military service as a centurion, captain, and now as a colonel! Who has received so many wounds from the enemy? No, they do not elect not me, but instead elect, Antisthenes — a merchant! Can you believe that! He has never been in the infantry in his life; nor have I ever heard that he accomplished any great feats in the cavalry. No! In fact, he has no real talent at all except to make money.*

Socrates. *Isn't his ability to make money a point in his favor? Surely, with the money he will be able to provide the troops with all the supplies that they need.*

Nicomachides. *Merchants are good hands at collecting money; but does that mean a merchant or trader would be able to command an army?*

Socrates. *But, Antisthenes is a man of great persistence; one who insists on winning, and that is a very necessary quality in a general.*

Haven't you noticed how each time he has been made chorus manager he has been successful, gaining superiority in each and every chorus?

Nicomachides. *Of course I have noticed, but there is a big difference between standing at the head of a band of singers and dancers and standing at the head of a troop of soldiers.*

Socrates. *Still, without any practical skill in singing or in the training of a chorus, Antisthenes somehow had the art to search out the best masters in these departments.*

Nicomachides. *Do you mean to imply, Socrates, that the man who finds success as a chorus manager will also find success with the army? Will he find masters to marshal the troops for him and others to fight his battles?*

Socrates. *If he seeks out the very best men in military affairs, just as he did when finding singers and trainers for his chorus, then it is very likely that he will be victorious. If he was willing to expend so much to win a choir victory for a single tribe, how much more will he expend to bring victory back to an entire state?*

Nicomachides. *Do you really mean, Socrates, that the same man, using the same functions, can manage a chorus well, and manage an army well?*

Socrates. *I mean that whatever a man manages, if he knows what he needs and is able to provide it, he will be a good manager — whether he is managing a chorus, a family, a business, or an army.*

Nicomachides. *I can't believe my ears Socrates! I would never have expected to hear you say that a good business man would make a good general.*

Socrates. *Let's examine their respective duties, and see if they are the same or different.*

Nicomachides. *Ok, let's do it.*

Socrates. *Well then, isn't a common duty of both to secure their command obedient and submissive?*

Nicomachides. *Certainly.*

Socrates. *And, shouldn't they also delegate to those best qualified to perform their distinctive tasks?*

Nicomachides. *Absolutely.*

Socrates. *Don't they also reprimand the bad and reward the good?*

Nicomachides. Decidedly.

Socrates. And, isn't it a noble ambition of both to win the kindly feeling of their subordinates?

Nicomachides. That too.

Socrates. And, do you consider it to the interest of both alike to win the loyalty of supporters and allies?

Nicomachides. Without a doubt.

Socrates. Is it not proper for both also to be careful of their resources?

Nicomachides. Very much so.

Socrates. Then, it equally concerns them both to be attentive and industrious in all of their respective endeavors?

Nicomachides. Yes, all these duties belong to both alike, but the parallel ends when you come to actual fighting.

Socrates. Yet both are sure to have enemies?

Nicomachides. There is no doubt about that.

Socrates. Then, should both be interested in getting the upper hand over these enemies?

Nicomachides. Certainly; but you still haven't told me what service organization and the art of management will be when it comes to actual fighting.

Socrates. Why, it is just at that moment, I believe, that they will be of most service. For the good economist knows that nothing is so advantageous or so lucrative as victory in battle; or, to put it negatively, nothing so disastrous and expensive as defeat. He will enthusiastically seek out and provide everything conducive to victory; he will painstakingly discover and guard against all that tends to defeat; and, when satisfied that all is ready and ripe for victory, he will deliver battle energetically. And, what is equally important, until the hour of final preparation has arrived, he will be cautious to deliver battle.

Do not despise men of economic genius, Nicomachides; the difference between the devotion requisite to private affairs and to affairs of state is merely one of quantity. For the rest the parallel holds strictly, and in this respect pre-eminently, that both are concerned with human instruments: which human beings, moreover, are of one type and temperament, whether we speak of devotion to public affairs or of the administration of private property. To fare well in either case is given to those who know the secret of dealing with humanity, whereas the absence of that knowledge will as certainly imply in either case a fatal note of discord. ---

This exchange suggests that management involves certain generic skills that can be viewed as universal. For example, a successful businessperson could successfully apply their skills to any endeavor including that of commanding an army. This is wrong. The fatal fundamental flaw is that of detachment, which leads to disinterest, which leads to ignorance of the enterprise under management.

Organizations do not make money, they engage in life. They provide goods and services that someone needs or wants. Further, every enterprise has people who not only understand the nuances of the enterprise as they progress from apprentice, to journeymen, to master but they also have the generic skills of management described and sold by Socrates. What becomes of these people and their motivation as outsiders are bought into an organization they did not build or understand? This only makes sense if there is a hidden agenda. That agenda can be theft of intellectual property to outright treachery as the true owners of an organization are sidelined and eventually removed.

So what is the role of management in a system driven organization? They are facilitators and information processing nodes. They are leaders and never bureaucrats. They should never polarize but bring together. They must be active stakeholders in the solution and may even provide significant input primarily from a holistic view rather than from a specialist view. They are mentors and developers of talent from apprentice to journeymen to master. They work with masters in development of talent. They should never ask what did you do for me today. There should never be a meeting where a manager goes around the table and asks what did you do for me today. The manager should know by making the appropriate rounds and being on top of the products. They should ask what are the issues and how can they facilitate the effort. They should help prioritize the issues, without filtering, then assign the resources within the team or contact the enterprise for additional resources outside the team. They have an obligation to detect technological and process short falls as the team attempts to provide its solutions. There is nothing more outrageous than to see people work with poor technology and process because management is too stupid or greedy to provide the resources needed to work effectively.

There are times, in extreme secrecy, where teams need to compartmentalize. In these cases management needs to be extremely enlightened and not driven by self-interest. Altruism needs to be the guiding principal. These environments by their very nature have few checks and balances and it is easy for national resources to be trapped on the equivalent of "The Island of Dr Mareau", with sick and corrupt management that may not be detected and checked for long periods of time.

Money is counted by the accounts. Managers just like staff work from goals rather than milestones. Accountants check and mark the milestones. Managers just like staff understand, own, develop, and update the technology and process. So they read and understand the Program or Project Evaluation and Review Technique (PERT) charts just like the staff and they create and update the same PERT charts with the staff.

So information processing node and facilitator is unique and key to their function. Anyone can count money and strip the assets until the inheritance is squandered.

Failure is Important

You know failure is important. You learn from failure. Those were the words from my WWII parents. I never understood those words until I saw the last 30 years unfold.

Without failure the envelope or challenge is too small. Without failure, because the challenge is too small, all progress stops. Without failure a generation of bullshit artists are born who always make sure they succeed no matter what the costs or the truth.

I was in my late 40's when my next manager arrived. His style was different; he would say, don't tell me the program details, go back to the program and work with the staff. I did not have the heart to tell him his judgement was poor and so his hand picked staff was stupid, arrogant, and nasty. I knew he was brilliant, but I did not realize how brilliant until his retirement and his educational background and interests surfaced. Although I eventually suspected what he was up to, he eventually told me - let them fail. The problem with that statement was I was an old guy and I was tired of being cannon fodder. However, the reality is he was right. These guys needed to fail and fail miserably. Only then could the organization get back on track and these guys progress to a different level. The problem is that strategy takes years and is extremely painful when 90% of the staff is stupid, arrogant, and nasty.

So there is a lesson. If a team needs to fail, then pull the innocent from the fray. If the team is good but the challenge is a true challenge, make sure the bullshit artists are kept away.

If things are grossly out of balance failure will eventually happen. In the USA the founders established a mode of limited government with terms in office and checks and balances. The thought being that if things get bad the terms in office will eventually expire. It is very sad if things do not self correct in a lifetime or within the term of a career. I am sure there were people who knew the folly of Germany or Russia in the last century, good people, but they were powerless to make the changes.

There is this movie called "AI". It is such a sad movie with many themes but one of the themes is about those who come after those who were before. Those who come after don't understand those who were before and long to know them yet they can not, except in some small way at the very end of the movie, but it's not enough. The point is these are our times and we should never squander our time with bullshit, lies, ignorance, arrogance, and just plain old nasty behavior. It is ok to fail if the challenge is a true challenge. We should only accept true challenges that have meaning and not waste our time and energy.

Performance Reviews

What are your values? What are your companies' values? What are your countries' values? What values do you want to pass to your children? What values do you want your children subjected to? What values did the rust belt industries have? What values did the high tech industries have? What values do the high tech industries have in this century? What values do outsource stakeholders have? What values do other countries, companies, cultures have?

Performance reviews represent the values that your organization thinks are important. It frames the behavior of all its members. So here are some performance measures in no particular order:

1. Creativity
2. Innovation
3. Invention
4. Leadership
5. Oral Communications
6. Written Communications
7. Competence
8. Professional Development
9. Productivity
10. Team Building
11. Team Work
12. Ability to Follow Orders
13. Ability to Maintain Control
14. Profit
15. Return on Investment

Take some time and order these performance measures, then compare them to your organization and country. Separate perception from reality. Separate the transmitted message from reality. A funny thing happened as the rust belt industries started to collapse in the 1970's. Slowly but surely the high tech industries started to change their values and Creativity, Innovation, Invention, Leadership started to disappear and were replaced by Productivity and Ability to Follow Orders.

Meanwhile there are serious problems that have been not addressed, as evidenced by the strong movement in Sustainable Development and the perception that something is terribly wrong. That perception also includes feelings that something has been lost. Some people state that we could never go to the Moon today and that maybe we never did go to the Moon.

Logic and Humanity

There is a television science fiction series from England that has been running on and off since 1962, "Dr Who". The thing about this TV show is that the Doctor is a very special being perhaps the most special being in the universe and yet he travels through space and time with a human companion.

As he travels he is called upon to solve incredible problems. But there is this significant issue. He can not solve the problems alone; he always needs a human companion. He knows the value of his human companion and often states that humans are his favorite life form and he loves humans. Aliens look upon humans as inferior in every way, from intelligence to physical characteristics. They ignore humans much like humans ignore ants. They know nothing of space travel, time travel, exotic science or the universe.

The Doctors' first companion was an average shop girl. His latest and greatest companion in this new century was also a shop girl and an average human, nothing special, and nothing brilliant. In the newest shows in this century, much is explained about humans the doctor loves. It appears as though some humans are very special and somehow they always know the right thing to do in any challenging situation. These decisions are not based on knowledge, special skills, or logic. These all-important decisions that allow the Doctor to succeed are based on the humanity of the companion.

So it is not about cold calculating logic. This smacks in the face of science and engineering. That is correct. That is why this book has two major sections Bachelor of Science and Bachelor of Arts. We can not ignore our humanity. It is our humanity coupled with our science that will allow us to save the universe, just like Doctor Who, the greatest scientist of all time and his human companion the embodiment of all that is human, the most noble of creations.

Spiritual Maturity

One of the major reasons I entered the high technology realm was because of my perception of spiritual immaturity in traditional industries, which eventually became the rust belt industries. My view was that the people were stupid, nasty, greedy, caddy, and that it was generally just a place to avoid for personal preservation. Somehow I knew there was a different way and I briefly found it in the high tech industries of the 1970's and early 80s'. That sounds arrogant and snobby. Hold that thought. Then something happened and others and I could see it but we were powerless to stop its expansion.

At the time I used to refer to it as the great nothing from the "Never Ending Story". But it was more complex than the loss of imagination. Perhaps it was the rise of arrogance, hubris, brutality, greed, vanity, slander, envy, pining in the high tech industry. Perhaps it was the rise of Darwinism over Symbiosis.

You should avoid these evils. Your acceptance of any of them can lead to a world where your children or their children will eat from the dirt and poop in the dirt. You get it.

Technology Is Not Always The Answer

In the early 1960's there were these strange human creatures that jumped around to the output of a 1 transistor AM radio playing music. They were called kids. In the early 2000's there were these strange human creatures that jumped around to the output of a 15 million-transistor cell phone playing music with less quality than the 1 transistor AM radio of the 60's. They were also called kids, but they were new kids.

Between the quantization distortion, non-linear audio compression expansion, digital compression, and network dropouts it is pathetic. Forget about the telephone quality of service issue and a little thing like peak load from Erlang. So what is wrong with this picture, besides being evil and predatory on an unsuspecting generation?

When I first started working I was quickly moved to the most elaborate highest technology environments of the day. That meant that I interfaced primarily with my parents' generation. These people were truly unbelievable. Yes it is true that many of them made terrible wars and practiced horrific genocide. We should never forget that group of low life humans. However there was another group in my parents generation that was just the opposite and gave me the modern world that I enjoyed and took for granted.

Anyway, when I worked with them they would sit down every so often and just start talking. I wish I could remember just 10% of those one way conversations I took for granted and thought would always exist. I can't remember their names and I can't remember their faces. I will say that some of the most brilliant people came from the old Federal Aviation Administration, before that agency was gutted by political agendas.

In any case one of the most unsettling one way conversations was when a man appeared in my office and started talking about air traffic control and systems. He talked and talked and talked and I would respond about how we could do it better.

He suddenly turned to me and said, "you know not all problems can be solved with technology".

Then he went on to say that technology needs to be carefully applied or it can do more harm than good. That totally blew me away. How could technology do harm? He then went on to say that it is the careful application of technology that made all the difference in the world. Careful application - I freaked out - how could you measure out and decide to slow down or speed up technology in the name of some type of good.

Those statements floored me and shook me to my core. I was part of the high tech generation. I firmly believed any problem could be solved with technology and because of that special knowledge I believed my generation would never repeat the mistakes of the past generations, the WW II and WWI generations and all those that preceded me and my peers - the stupid generations.

Well guess what, technology can not solve all problems. The use of 15 million transistors to replace a 1-transistor device with less quality is insane. It is a gross misuse of resources. Granted it was all in the name of wireless personal two-way communications, but there is still something wrong with this picture.

A generation later we have a system that really is less capable than the previous systems that were tied with wires and AM FM transmitters. How many people really need to reach out and touch someone while walking down the aisle of a super market? Did the previous generation really have problems finding a telephone when needed? What was the need for emergency communications and has anything really changed in terms of emergency response. What price did we pay? Does it matter that we lost AT&T Bell labs and other related research labs? How will you feel when all the telephone landlines are gone? How will you feel when all the radio stations are gone? If you want to know, go visit a third world country.

So technology is not always the answer. Nor is chasing money which is supposed to spur technology through random competition always the answer.

Approaches From Our Civilization

There are many different ways to solve problems. What are those ways - techniques - methods - tools that we humans have used in the past 5000 years to solve problems?

In the early 2000's a tool was created to analyze technical specification text. Its purpose was to help in the authoring of requirement text. As part of its operation, it allowed a user to create analysis rules using concepts based on the Internet search engine. It also allowed a user to profile a document by mining and counting word instances.

One day this tool was applied to a document from the European Union on global warming, "Green Paper a European Strategy for Sustainable, Competitive and Secure Energy". Much to everyone's surprise meaningful insights surfaced from the analysis and new rules were created. The tool was then applied to the "Stern Review: The Economics of Climate Change" from the UK, once again there was meaningful output and new rules were created. It was finally applied to the "Climate Change Technology Program Strategic Plan" from the United States, and something very important happened.

The participants started to create rules that attempted to identify and characterize how humans solve problems. This was based on the knowledge of the team and research on the Internet trying to find techniques for solving problems. This all fell under the umbrella of trying to analyze policy documents.

The first thing that surfaced was the idea of broad approaches to solving problems like Markets, Technology, Education, Science, Government, People, International Efforts, Engineering, and Systems.

The next thing that surfaced was the realization that there were categories of approaches - tools - techniques - methods - processes for solving problems like Institutions, Societal Approaches, Organizational Tools, Nation State Tools, and International Tools.

Then it was realized there were other aspects of policy document analysis like Social Warnings, National Roles, International Roles, and Special Interests.

This is an example of technology running amok and actually yielding progress in many areas. The first was an attempt to try to quantify and characterize documents that were deemed very political with no redeeming content. It was found that the documents did not have a political agenda and were actually representations of different levels of maturity on the subject. The second was an attempt to study history and try to identify and categorize how humans solve problems using real approaches.

What is interesting is if someone actually runs the tool on the three documents, they as tool users actually change. They are more able to discern rhetoric from real statements of possible solutions in a political speech. In other words they are able to more easily separate bullshit from honest attempts to address problems using traditional techniques and tools known throughout history. They become more critical and able to discern higher quality from the incoming signals.

The following is just a list of the rules and some details that are authored in the policy analysis tool:

- <u>Broad Approaches</u>: Markets, Technology, Education, Science, Government, People, International, Engineering, Systems, Alternatives
- <u>Institutions</u>: Academia, Government, Industry, Labs, Think, Tanks, NGO, Non, Profits, Popular, Media, Technical, Media, Associations
- <u>Societal Approaches</u>: Peaceful, Sacrifice, Stressed, Violent
- <u>Organizational Tools</u>: Technical, Process, Management, Gestalts, Implementation
- <u>Nation State Tools</u>: Policy, Legislate, Regulate, Deregulate, Tax, Military, Departments, Resources, Proactive, Transparency
- <u>International Tools</u>: Policy, Resources, Proactive
- <u>Social Warnings</u>: General, Human, Anger, Environment, Health, Economic, Earth
- <u>National Roles</u>: Religion, Defense, Money, Wealth, Education, Agriculture, Health, State, People, Labor
- <u>International Roles</u>: People, Government, Industry, International, Academia, Community, Money, Time
- <u>Special Interests</u>: Defense, Intelligence, Food, Health, Pharmaceuticals, Chemicals, Mining, Energy
- <u>Emotions</u>: Happy, Sad, Love, Hate, Fear

- <u>Overall Reaction</u>: Positive, Negative

The point is that generations upon generations of humans have actually identified thousands of approaches to solve problems. These approaches should always be revisited and expanded upon with each new challenge. In fact technology might even help us to determine if we have exhausted our current list of approaches to a challenging problem.

Memory and Generation Gap

At one time there was this thing called the generation gap. For some reason I detect less of a generation gap today than in the past. Is that because we have slowed down progress? Is the modern world here with nothing new to follow?

I am fascinated by some of the works of the previous generation.

There is a bridge that connects Philadelphia and New Jersey called the Benjamin Franklin Bridge and it was opened in 1929. In 1929 there was not much going on in South Jersey. Why was this massive bridge created? What was guiding these people to build a thing that not only lasted decades but also had the capacity to support our modern world in 2007 that could never have been justified in the 1920's?

We all listen to music. The same, what ever it is, holds true for music. I am fascinated to read about the old magnetic studio recorders that measured and adjusted speed on the fly to achieve incredible levels of reproduction. Because of this we can listen to music from the 50's and 60's that in many cases sounds better than music recorded today. What pushed these people to achieve this level of quality? Did they record music for extremely rich people like Howard Hughes and their custom sound systems?

I remember the generation gap like it was yesterday. I remember how the Beatles were viewed as new in 1964 and how that music was new, not part of the WWII generation. Now that the decades have gone by I see that members of the Beatles and their kind have started to pass away with people I equated with the old generation. In some cases one could argue the old generation lived a bit longer than the new generation, but still something very important happened. I realized these people were all of the same generation. They were all my parents and they all shared this same incredible devotion to quality and work. The Beatles worked their asses off, just like the guys working in the factory. Just like the guys in the factory that always thought of new ways to do things better the Beatles thought of new ways in music.

Post WWII American and British culture became very valuable products as the world embraced these entertainment products. When the USA fell on hard times in the last century, Sony bought large quantities of USA entertainment licensing rights.

Fast forward to the 1990's there was this TV series called "Dark Skies". It essentially set all the major events from the end of WWII through to the 1960's in a conspiracy alien agenda. It had great images and music from that time. For years fans have been demanding a DVD set of Dark Skies and Sony made plans for such a release. Sony Entertainment cancelled the release, because of prohibitive music licensing costs even though they own vast areas of this USA product but now world wide cultural heritage.

Copyrights were originally set at 28 years, the expected lifetime of the original artist, not a corporate entity, or the family descendents. Copyright laws in the USA have recently been modified to exceed 95 years in an effort to protect the residuals of Mickey Mouse.

So what is my point here? Where is the generation gap? Why are people longing for the past? Why does the Ben Franklin Bridge exist? Would our bridge today be just 2 lanes with regulations identifying when you can drive on the bridge and price incentives where costs would be prohibitive for normal work time commutes? This is important stuff and what right do we have to deny the world of music from our parents' time.

Freedom and Liberty

In 1980 the world was treated to Carl Sagans the "COSMOS" television series, a spectacular work of art with many themes. One of his strongest themes was that of freedom and liberty. How freedom and liberty are the prerequisites for discovery.

This is everywhere. It permeates our cultures because it is

inalienable it comes from the creator. You can't take it away; you have no right to take it away. As I sit here trying to determine which words to type I am watching an old movie "Red River" where this struggle surfaces. John Wayne loses his way and wants ultimate control on every aspect of everything unfolding in the chain of events. Montgomery Clift sees his adopted fathers' failures and after confirmation from Walter Brennan, takes matters into his own hands. In the end they both reconcile as John Wayne realizes his mistake and Montgomery Clift realizes John wanted him to be molded in the heat of fire to emerge as a jewel. In the end you see John draw the symbol of the ranch which has a big D on one side for his name. He then takes his stick and draws a big M on the other side and his closing words are "you earned it". This is classic stuff and I have 52 years of film, television, music, books, theatre, and life that have constantly shown me this struggle so that I would never lose my way. Interestingly John Wayne was a staunch conservative and Montgomery Clift was a staunch liberal. They both agreed not to talk politics on the set before the job started and that is what happened. Their performances were great as they worked in a flawless team.

"Les Misérables the Musical" opened on Broadway in 1987. There is a scene where Marius Pontmercy, Jean Valjeans future adopted son in law looks down on the mess of his time and declares - where have all the leaders gone. Don't lose that thought, ever. Freedom and liberty have a price.

Just because someone or something says you are free and you have liberty does not make it so. Your parents may have been free and enjoyed liberty. Your children may be free and enjoy liberty. What about you and your compatriots, freedom and liberty ever enter into your discussions.

One day I was in the office of a WWII person, Hal. Dr. Hal was a national resource. Things were not going well as the Howard Hughes Medical Institute was ordered by the IRS to divest itself of Hughes Aircraft and GM was eyeing fabulous assets to strip. Hal raised his head from behind his desk piled with papers and said, as I understood it: - *This is not a democracy. Companies are not democracies. They are autocratic and you follow orders no matter how stupid they are my way or the highway.* -

Have you ever had your technical papers edited and the editing left you angry? Have you ever had your slides edited and the editing left you angry? Have you ever had someone take your slides and present them only to see they were clueless about the content? Have you ever had someone take your papers, your words and put their name on it because they were your manager and then see the stakeholders not even acknowledge you. This happened at every company and organization I was associated with except the FAA, MITRE and a Contraves division in the USA, all non-profits or government.

The problem with the FAA was, as a federal employee I could never run for a public office. I was aware of this because of a history class in 8th grade where I actually read the struggle of civil servants prior to the great depression. This was one of the laws passed to stop political patronage. It was used to establish a career track. In any case when I actually started working as a federal employee, that always bothered me. It was one of the excuses I used to leave my job and retirement in an R&D setting - a career. Don't get me wrong, there were other reasons like not enough money to allow me to raise a family as privatization was kicking in. So freedom and liberty are rather complex and yet every blade of grass on earth can grow the way it wants to grow, but people restrict, control, smother, and even kill other people because freedom and liberty get in the way of an agenda.

There is no excuse for behavior that attacks the rights bestowed by the creator. The price is always the same and eventually people in this trap will see themselves in great need and want as natural forces go to work. Those forces extinguish creativity, innovation, and invention as people just stop, they stop, as they realize truth will get them nowhere and may even kill them or their families.

Just one more quote from the movie Flashdance, it was on TV the same day as Red River. "Don't you understand when you give up your dream you die". Are you surrounded by dead people, are you dead?

Magic and Serendipity

Magic or Serendipity does happen. It happens when you least expect it. You never know it's magic when you are in the moment but you know something special is happening and you have no control but it is good. Sometimes you can recognize serendipity. Neither happens often, so it is a big deal.

Learn to recognize magic in different groups when it happens. Try not to kill the magic for others, do not be jealous of the magic, and do not try to steal the magic. Magic transforms a path. A whole New World surfaces and becomes available when magic happens. The same holds true for Serendipity. It's amazing how the universe somehow throws people together without anyone running a master plan and that group is very special.

Love

Nothing of great value gets done without love. If something great happened, it is because someone had love of what they were doing. The more love the greater the accomplishment. It is not about motivation, money, greed, fear, or anything except for love.

If you ignore love, extinguish love you kill life in your architecture, process, solution, innovation, creativity, engineering, technology, science - you destroy your universe. Love is what will get the team through all hurtles and punch through to new levels of understanding.

Don't confuse passion with love. Passion is only the start of love. The more people yell at each other and the more they can freely express their ideas the more chance there is for full love to surface. It is a sign that they are starting to fall in love with what they are doing. As all barriers drop and the real magic of humans changing their world surfaces the closer the team approaches truth and the real solutions start to surface. Love is the essence of the power of our humanity as we strive to make a better world.

Did I mention the Beatles? Never ever betray anyone's love.

Diplomacy

At this point you are either with me or against me. In the latter case you need to call upon your diplomacy skills to make progress or is it political skills.

There used to be a concept of solutions where everybody wins. Today that is frowned upon and if you go down that path you may lose your job. This is a recent trend and a result of a naïve generation that thinks in terms of only winners and losers and the hell with the losers. The reality is the WWII generation came out of their hole by using the simple concept of letting everyone win. It is hard work to find solutions where everyone benefits.

Respect and being humble is key to any diplomatic effort. Without this simple characteristic all progress stops. The one who has no respect and is not humble may think they win, but in the end they will lose because the optimal solution is never surfaced in that environment. It is predatory Darwinian thinking where everyone gets killed except for the last eating pig. That winner soon dies of starvation. It is about Symbiosis.

When people make a mistake and they realize it, you have to give them a way out so that dignity is preserved. The problem is many people want a face saving way out without realizing the error of their follies. They only return to cause more havoc.

Doctorate

Something happened after WWII. There was a great emphasis on science and engineering. Eventually you will read the famous paper to President Roosevelt from DR. Vannevar Bush. This paper was so important because it set the policy and tone for science, education, and engineering. As a result millions of people had the opportunity to study and enter these fields. I had the opportunity to become an Electrical Engineer and cross the country a few times working in government, non-profits, industry, and some international efforts.

My first job was with the FAA at a research facility called National Aviation Facilities Experimental Center (NAFEC). Even today I miss the environment of NAFEC, the easygoing people, the massive laboratories. I do not miss the low pay or some people who in the past suggested I go live in a trailer. Especially after I worked so hard to get my BSEE. Today that place is called the FAA Technical Center. I found it fascinating that people of all educational and skill levels worked in this same massive resource.

My second job was at Hughes Aircraft. There was no question I thought I had arrived. It was so massive even after my stay at NAFEC on its 5000 acres I was still intimidated. Within the first 30 days I voiced my concern about not having an advanced degree, I was just a lowly BSEE. My immediate supervisor turned to me and laughed. He said Hughes is a very different place. We are not into formality or credentials we are into what people can do. Within a few years you will have the equivalent of a few Ph.Ds. under your belt. I did not believe him and I felt uneasy. Little did I know he was correct as I was breaking new ground in computer architectures, system engineering, analysis techniques, and process. Funny, eventually I felt arrogance and hubris got the best of me, but what really happened was Hughes Aircraft started to disappear from under my feet.

So this section is a very advanced area of this book. This is your opportunity to earn your doctorate based on my previous work. If you can formalize your thesis in a university setting, that's ok, but what we really need is for you to do this work in effective institutions that will push the state of the art in Sustainable Development. I hope that my work in this small book will start to fire up these institutions where you can do this. Good luck and have fun.

Science versus Liberal Arts

First of all it is not liberal arts versus science or science versus liberal arts but science and liberal arts or liberal arts and science. One without the other can not solve difficult problems. Organizations become ineffective if one is left out of the mix.

In many ways the introduction of the computer has done more damage to society than we know because it has removed whole groups of people with liberal arts backgrounds who were given the tasks of publication and editing in high technology organizations. Many had broad and deep backgrounds in philosophy, history, and the arts, which allowed them to surface in sophisticated organizations and make major contributions to the major solutions of the last 50 years that we now all enjoy.

Today liberal arts people are only found in management and that is not where they should be as they detach themselves from the business at hand with little or no understanding of the real challenges and no motivation to jump into the fray. In fact they are only used to manipulate hidden agendas as vested interests attempt to maintain status quo. A classic example is stripping of assets of organizations that took decades to develop. Enough of us have lived through this scenario to realize we are not in the middle of normal rise peak and decline of technology, product, or an industry. So the introduction of the computer was a big deal and not all of it was good.

The big question is how do we reintroduce liberal arts people back into high technology organizations. In additional, there is another related challenge.

We have had formal System Engineering degree programs for a number of years. We also had companies engaged in this thing called systems and system engineering. As I have traveled across the USA, I have only met a handful of System Engineers and in all cases they worked for one of these "system houses" they never came from a University or another kind of organization trying to stamp out a System Engineer. These people were academically very strong and usually EE sometimes ME sometimes Philosophy and cooked in these great system engineering organizations.

The problem is there is this push to stamp someone as an expert with a certification. Tests and certifications remind me of companies that provide you a test that you must pass before you come to work in their software shop. The tests ask questions like what is polymorphism and inheritance. These companies are clueless and waste precious resources, mostly people. However they do continue to get funded.

I detect a similar scenario unfolding for systems as for the software crisis - certain classes of companies / organizations pushing for these fast solutions to make a quick buck with zero risk and investment. This is a devastating turn of events. It is time to start doing engineering again.

We have about 38 years worth of infrastructure engineering to catch up on in the USA alone. How old is the space shuttle? Now we have new constraints because some are now more aware of managing resources (global warming). This will require people with very high levels of consciousness not people who know the difference between polymorphism and inheritance on an employment test. It will require system engineers like those that gave us radio, television, telephones, freeways (yes they are free), air transport, etc. These things did not just happen randomly. They were not done by people with quick jump start lets start making money off this body so lets give it a training fix.

Sorry for being so caustic but this is critical stuff. I keep seeking truth and sometimes it offends. That is not my intent. Education is the key to really starting to create those wonderful system engineers we so desperately need in the next 100 years. That education is formal via Universities and informal cooking on the job as apprentice's transition to true masters.

What is Creative System Engineering

So to go back to the Introduction. . .

Imagine a place where you create things and make decisions where there are no hidden agendas and all stakeholders are treated equally. How would potential approaches surface, how would they be narrowed and selected, how would decisions be made. What tools and techniques would be used if they were not the greatest moneyed interests, the most politically powerful, or the most dangerous?

How about the scientific method using reasonable techniques understood by reasonable people in a process that is fully transparent and visible to everyone. Everyone has a view of all the alternatives. Everyone has a view of all the decision paths. Everyone has an opportunity to impact the alternatives and decision paths. Do not fall for the rhetoric that this is mob rule or design by committee. These are reasonable people using 5000 plus years of tools, techniques, processes, and methods to make informed decisions. There are no hidden agendas with vested interests or people who just give up and go silent or worse compromise. Everyone is comfortable with the decision because it is intuitively obvious to all. Everyone obviously has responsibility in such an endeavor. No one can blow off that responsibility.

That in a nutshell is Creative System Engineering. This book hopefully will provide the framework for us to start practicing this "dying" art.

Creative System Engineering is not new. Education, Science, and Engineering were the pillars that were used to create a spectacular world after WWII. These pillars literally allowed us to go to the Moon. The great system engineering projects were all implemented with massive internal education, massive new science, and massive new engineering. This resulted in creative system solutions that changed our world forever. The genie was let out of the bottle and the world has never been the same. This simple book just applied the word Creative to System Engineering to represent the previous century technique used on system engineering programs that changed our world for the better in ways we can not imagine. All we can do is look back in amazement.

System Engineering versus Management

You are either a system engineering driven organization or a management driven organization. It is impossible to be both. In a management driven organization, management always has the power of final say regardless of the science, engineering, findings, and tradeoffs. In fact management decisions may be hidden and can include any agenda including those that devastate the solution that will work.

Ok So What Do I Do From Beginning to the End

There is an old saying, keep it simple stupid. What is buried in this is genius. The sheer act of genius takes the complex and makes it simple. I did not invent this. This was practiced in the last century at remarkable places.

1. Identify the system boundary and why it is the boundary
2. Identify your key requirements and why you selected them (top 10)
3. Identify your key issues and why you selected them (top 10)
4. Identify your alternatives and why you selected them (7 plus or minus 2)
5. Draw a picture of each alternative (1 page)
6. Succinctly state the essence of each alternative (1 page and a list of 5-9 bullets)
7. Do a tradeoff of each alternative (including support for 100 years, etc)
8. Apply science and engineering to each spin of the tradeoff (don't cook the books)
9. Identify how you will build each approach (process, methods, tools, etc)
10. Build a proof of concept prototype (from paper to computer simulations to physical models)
11. Mature the prototype at a small operational setting (try it before you make a mistake)
12. Roll out the solution to the infrastructure (slowly and learn)
13. There is beauty in diversity (nothing wrong with multiple approaches and companies)

Do this like your life depends on it. Do it out of love of the technology, family, country, planet, universe, and the creator.

Institutions and Companies to Avoid

What institutions and companies should be avoided? Everything that exists today, nothing is working.

Our current institutions are a direct result of the Reagan revolution and trying to deal with the perceived problems of the 1970's. The Reagan revolution has failed. Government did not get smaller it was privatized. It is bigger than it ever was and falls into the classic definition of fascism where government and corporations have become one. Empowerment of the individual has gone in the opposite direction. People have less power today across the board to influence decisions and their lives. Examples include the franchising of traditional small family businesses to removal of budget authority from working staff in corporations. Management is seen as the magic bullet somehow directing the most educated, engaged, self actuated generation in history.

The price has been enormous and it is loss of creativity, innovation and invention in every aspect of society but mostly from the high tech industries. We have converted our traditional high tech beacons of leadership into rust belt feeble attempts to make money, now, and for me, not you. Do not confuse miniaturization, an echo of the previous world, with progress.

It is time for a recovery plan. That recovery plan needs to include what it means now that the Berlin Wall has come down. Back to the WWII generation. They would say to me - you know the one who loses the cold war may not actually lose the cold war as both sides spend their way into oblivion. The first one to say enough, I am done, may be less bankrupt than the second, allowing the first to recover, as the second completely collapses.

After 20 years we have yet to establish a plan to transition our defense industry. We now have companies that derive 100% of their revenues from defense. These companies think they are in business. They have executives making millions. Prior to this shift, defense companies were non-profits or divisions of commercial companies who felt it was their patriotic duty to have defense divisions. The examples are respectively Hughes Aircraft and RCA. Now after privatization we also have new companies with 100% of their revenues derived from non-defense government services and operations.

After the Berlin wall came down legislation should have been passed which should have mandated that no company can derive 100% of their revenues from the government. After a 5-year period, which would have been sometime in the 1990s, their revenues should have been capped at 50% from government sources. Each of these companies should have put together a recovery plan to take them into a post cold war era. There is no legislation and no defense company has such a plan. Further, we have a plethora of new companies offering privatized services to the government that can not exist in a commercial setting.

Meanwhile we have real work to do in this new century. It is called Sustainable Development. I know our kids and their kids want a world they can enjoy. It's not just about my immediate gratification and me.

Warning and Responsibility

The communists won. The fascists won. The capitalists won. The socialists won. It is not about communists, fascists, capitalists, and socialists. It is about elitists. They exist everywhere in all times, that is why the American Experiment of checks and balances is so important. It is a simple idea and we know it works. We know it saves us when the elitists take over and do massive damage.

It was only 100 years ago that our ancestors were pooping and eating from the dirt. Watch what you say and do. This is your time, live it well.

An Inconvenient Truth

The following is my response on a technical message board submission where the topic was - you guessed it - An Inconvenient Truth.

--- *I said I would respond in about a week to the movie "An Inconvenient Truth". I noticed that there are still some people talking with great authority that did not see the movie. Oh well, it has been long enough to see the movie. . .*

So here it is, my view of the movie and this subject, and why I think this is so important for those engaged in system engineering.

In the last century or two there were people who tried to find a different way. In the process we were introduced to massively powerful new technologies like radio, TV, airplanes, and automobiles. All these technologies allowed even the most uninitiated to gain an "education". Some would call this education a liberal arts education. My formal education was technical in electrical engineering. We, us engineers, were always "told" that we lacked the "other education(s)" even though I seemed to be able to address all subjects. In my early professional years I thought it was because of my strong high school background. Now I know different. It's the legacy of all the music, movies, TV, magazines, some books, travel, and time that has allowed me to get a greater and broader education than Benjamin Franklin.

So even though we are engineers mathematicians, scientists, with a few philosophy majors thrown in the mix, there is no reason for us to not understand what the movie "An Inconvenient Truth" is about, unless we did not see the movie. So if you did not see the movie and I peaked your interest, stop here. . .

The title of the movie is "An Inconvenient Truth". It is not called "Global Warming" or "Environmentalists Unite" or "Al Gore, Let Me Tell You about Global Warming". It is called "An Inconvenient Truth". The movie has 4 stories.

The first story is about Al Gore. It is about his life and how he got involved in politics and now Global Warming.

The second story is about his family and how their beautiful farm that they all loved "helped" to kill their "daughter" and his sister. The difficulty the father had in coming to grips with the truth about his farm, the horrible "Inconvenient Truth", that led him to stop farming tobacco. The "Inconvenient Truth" that led Al to understand why the farm, which he loved is now dormant.

The third story is about life in Washington DC. The "Inconvenient Truth" that none of representatives are interested in "truth" only their special interests. So although Al did not say it, he got tired of all the BS (bullshit) as everyone pushed their agenda, no matter how wrong it was because the "Truth was Inconvenient".

"On Bullshit" from Princeton professor Harry G. Frankfurt, Winner of the 2005 Bestseller Awards, Philosophy Category:
  http://www.pupress.princeton.edu/titles/7929.html

After seeing the movie it's easy to understand why he states he is out of politics. He got tired of all the BS, it was hopeless, and he is going in a different direction to make his contribution. He is lucky because he has the money to do it, unlike many others who are "trapped" with the "idiots".

The fourth story was about global warming. But within the framework of the movie, global warming is irrelevant if we have a people and their systems that are not interested in finding truth. If you can find truth then you can solve problems.

The "special people" from the previous generation had to find truth many times. Because of this we enjoy our modern world. It's not hard if you are willing to keep asking questions. When the right questions eventually surface, the solutions are always self-evident. That is what I was told decades ago, and that is how I operated until about 1987. Somewhere in that time frame truth in my engineering world disappeared, which was tragic because as a system engineer that is all I do, seek truth.

So there you have it, a small phrase in the last paragraph. As a system engineer I seek truth.

System engineering is the only discipline that tries to seek truth. It is not specialized. It tries to take in the whole picture. What has happened since Hughes Aircraft has disappeared, a non profit corporation, is that "companies" have created the "system engineer" position and assigned "a system engineer" to each project then claimed they use system engineering, implying that their solutions are based on "truth".

So our profession is a great profession. I feel it includes the ranks of those like Benjamin Franklin. Our profession is probably in a unique position to address this major problem, "global warming", because we seek truth. The problem is there are no more system engineering based institutions. Hughes Aircraft is gone. The Federally Funded Research and Development Facilities (FFRDC) go to congress every year to get re-funded, so they just dance to the whims of congress. The companies think system engineering is about finding someone with "system engineer" on their resume and have them (one person) write all those useless specifications and studies (done by hundreds of people in the past) that no one will read.

So fundamentally I don't think we have any institutions left to even address something like creating radio, TV, airports, highway interstates, or Global Warming and what it implies. We just have a few "old system engineers" who remember seeing a different way. The way included "round tables" with participants from many perspectives. The application of anything in our world (any technology, technique, formula, created in the past 5000 years, and even etc) to help surface the questions, surface the alternatives, study the differences in the alternatives, and optimize the final solutions. The FFRDCs can't do it, forget about the companies, universities can't do it, and places like Hughes Aircraft (non profits beholding to no one) are gone because they were deemed to be dangerous in the 80's (sorry I strayed). Not that Hughes was a panacea.

Today if you ask any "inconvenient questions" you will be inundated with BS (propaganda) and get fired. With little hope of future employment in your previous field. So I am not sure how Al Gore and his friends hope to tackle this project, because except for system engineers, and their loose ties, there are no "impartial institutions" left to address the problem.

So do I believe in Global Warming? The question is almost irrelevant on a personal basis. It is about policy and resources. Is there sufficient evidence to warrant the study of this subject? As a system engineer I need to take an impartial view until I have the evidence. However I may decide that irrespective of global warming the subject might force me to rethink how I live in my house and how I set my dinner table. For example, would I place waste material next to my food and drink?

If I accept the premise of global warming, then I have to take an impartial view of the potential solutions. But who will develop these alternative solutions? Who will bring all the current "stakeholders together" at a round table? Who will establish a system engineering division of 2000 people (sorry, Hughes Fullerton had 2,000 people in the system engineering division)? Assuming that Hughes was still around, how would they even roll out the solutions, through legislation?

So the "Inconvenient Truth" is not that we have global warming, but that we have no institutions to address this problem, except for the discipline of system engineering.

So there you have it, a creative system engineering challenge for the next 100 years. The biggest project in human history. Starting with recommendations on the types of institutions to establish that may have a slim hope of effectively addressing this problem.

So, what is the problem, what is the truth? It's obvious. It is not about Global Warming. It is about always maximizing the effective use of our resources and making life better here on earth.

Now go see the movie. ---

Technical Emergence

Yet another one of my messages from a technical message board. The topic was finding the unexpected.

--- Wow. This is where the kids are separated from the grown-ups. You hit the nail on the head with the simple statement "finding the unexpected".

So let me give you a real world example. When I started working the old timers talked about the automation of the USA air traffic control system. This was when the computer was introduced. They, the FAA, originally thought that automation would allow them to reduce the staff. In reality the number of people in the system significantly increased as people thought of new ways of using this new automation in air traffic control. The whole air traffic control system was punched to a whole new level, a level unimaginable prior to its introduction, and it was allowed to move to that level.

Let's fast-forward a few years with the same system from the FAA. When new features / levels of automation were added the work would begin on paper, progress to mathematical computer simulations, then move into simulation labs that would emulate field sites. If it survived these simulations one or more key sites would be picked and they would try the automation during off peak times when air traffic was light. After the key sites shook out the new feature it would then be rolled out to the infrastructure. If there was political pressure for a new feature the simulation lab would be bypassed and the key sites would simultaneously have to make the thing work and fit it into the real world setting. This is the mother load of system engineering. This costs serious money and it is not for idiots. This is serious business and this is how the FAA worked at one time.

Let's now talk about something we can all relate to like

genetically modified corn. How do you go about finding the unexpected in this case? What does it mean if you cross a tomato with a blue bird gene and a human gene? There is no key site testing or is there? When do you stop the computer simulations? How much money do you spend on the analysis - $1 billion, $10 billion, $100 billion assuming that more money will allow more human eyes and perspectives to view the problem and find unintended consequences?

So it would be nice to predict the unexpected, but if you could predict it then it would not be unexpected. What you can do is turn on the analysts and track their rate of discoveries of unexpected behaviors over time. You could then hope that you asymptotically approach a very small rate of discovery. But, as we all know, the funding can modulate the discovery rate. So you need a mature people and organization to also determine the sensitivity rate based on funding.

This is one of the hearts of real system engineering. This is why management and the pinheads try to stop this incredible technique.

The dirty little secret is that with the computer revolution most solutions have turned into large system solutions. The big question is can the system do damage or cause loss of life as it operates? If it can, then these practitioners who state "Systems Engineering is just for those multi-billion dollar defense programs. Stay away from me with that stuff" need to be made aware of their liabilities. They then have a choice; they can do proper engineering or engage in "other practices".

A few years ago I created a tool to help authors write specification text. As I enticed associates to take it for a spin around the block I also worked with using the tool on various test cases. Something emerged.

But before that emergence, the tool itself was an emergence. This tool uses an APACHE server, web browser, and this engine I created using PERL. I wrapped the whole thing so that it runs on the user computer and installs like a regular PC application. Essentially I use the Internet technology to analyze an engineering specification. This is an unintended consequence of the Internet tools (APACHE, web browser, and PERL).

Now the tool itself displayed an interesting emergent property. Everyone that used the tool started to think of new applications, both in and out of engineering. In the engineering world I thought I created a front-end system-engineering tool to help people write clean specs. NASA grabbed the thing for a study and applied it to the IV&V phase. Other people suggested that it could be used during concept time to mine analysis studies. Others stated QA and Test could use it. Yet others stated you could use it to mine documents of similar systems to help develop the current system.

I took the tool and pushed it into other applications and industries. One area I pushed it into is the analysis of policy documents and I used it to analyze some documents on Global Warming and Sustainable Development.

I always felt that new technology based solutions had the greatest levels of positive emergence and that those positive characteristics always out weighed the negative emergence. I think this tool based on new technology is an example of that relationship. ---

Non Technical Emergence

Getting back to the FAA and its approach to rolling out system upgrades and new solutions. The approach described above was practiced prior to 1980. It was branded, as a costly approach that did not allow the system to evolve as solutions would rarely progress from paper through to simulation labs out to the key sites. Many solutions would spend years in the simulation labs only to be rejected by the operational staff at the key sites.

The approach circa 1980 was to gather up these R&D programs sitting on the shelf and incorporate them into the Brown Book or National Airspace Plan (NAS) plan. This was a blue print that would take the FAA into the 21st century. One of the largest programs in that plan was the Advanced Automation System (AAS). That program was a failure and the FAA has essentially missed 25 years worth of upgrades, things that were sitting in R&D labs in the 1970's. There were some successes such as the eventual roll out of Mode-s and Voice Switching Communication System (VSCS). But the key system the AAS failed.

In an environment of the best of intentions and attempts to practice system engineering at its finest, something emerged on the AAS program. The emergence was massive political strife.

There were two companies that led huge teams that were selected for a design competition, Hughes Aircraft and IBM Federal Systems Group. Both teams knew that they were supposed to make the R&D programs real and build upon this R&D realizing emergence would surface. The Hughes team proposed a modern fully distributed architecture. It was my architecture. I put all the ideas from NAFEC to work on a system where all the tracking functions would be pushed to the common console. So in many ways it was the FAA architecture born from R&D at NAFEC. Curiously during architecture presentations, Hughes took my words and architecture and let other people present it to the FAA while I presented the centralized or IBM architecture to the FAA. The IBM team proposed a centralized architecture based on their primary product, mainframe computers. Needless to say IBM was awarded the production contract even though the Hughes solution was deemed as superior. IBM then failed to deliver after a few billion dollars.

Now here is what *Emerged*.

Hughes was a non profit organization. Howard Hughes established a medical foundation in 1953 and donated Hughes Aircraft to the Howard Hughes Medical Institute. They were given a very broad charter, which included the study of the "genesis of life itself" in Hughes' words.

Rumor was that in 1967 a law was passed where foundations could not own more than 10% of a stock. For whatever reason Hughes Aircraft was left alone and allowed to address the defense needs of the USA while donating small profits to the Medical Institute and plowing R&D money back into the operation. It had grown into one of the largest employers in the southwest and employed the largest number of engineers and electrical engineers in the country. They also had the largest ratio of engineers, which was in the 60-70% range if my memory serves me. Then something happened and the Medical Institute was directed to divest Hughes aircraft in the early 1980's. By 1985 Hughes Aircraft became the property of General Motors. The purchase was executed on December 20, 1985 for approximately $5.2 billion, $2.7 billion in cash and the rest in 50 million shares of GM Class H stock.

This had a huge impact on the company. It was so significant that

I left for greener pastures. This is probably why the company was unable to secure the AAS production program and IBM was given the go ahead by the FAA. So the emergence was the unexpected massive change in status of Hughes Aircraft. Who would have thought that something as stable and massive as Hughes Aircraft would have been dismantled? It actually took an act of the United States Government, the same government that it was servicing. Chalk this up to privatization, deregulation, and reducing the size of government as the political shifts away from the New Deal started to happen within the country.

Hughes spanned every aspect of every technology. At the time its revenues were approximately $6 billion per year with Fullerton producing approximately $1.2 billion per year. Coincidentally the budget of the FAA was about $6 billion per year and the IBM research budget was about $6 billion per year with revenues around $40-$50 billion. The medical foundation in the last year of my employment received $250 million that year. At the time I never made the connection that all of Hughes Aircraft was an R&D organization and so its R&D was comparable to IBM. IBM would manufacture and Hughes would subcontract manufacturing when possible. Four times a year Hughes Aircraft California operations would publish a phone book with names and locations. It was one-inch thick using 8-point font in three columns. At the back was a yellow-pages of various products and services. Here is a list of the Hughes sites that illustrate the breath and depth of this organization:

Corporate Offices: Culver City, CA

Electro-Optical & Data Systems Group Divisions:
```
Electro-Optical Engineering-----El Segundo, CA
Manufacturing-------------------El Segundo, CA
Space Sensors-------------------El Segundo, CA
Strategic Systems---------------El Segundo, CA
Tactical Systems----------------El Segundo, CA
Technology Support--------------El Segundo, CA
```

Ground Systems Group Divisions:
```
Communications & Radar----------Fullerton, CA
Data Processing Products--------Fullerton, CA
```

```
Engineering Services & Support--Fullerton, CA
Manufacturing-------------------Fullerton, CA
Software Engineering------------Fullerton, CA
Systems-------------------------Fullerton, CA
```

Industrial Electronics Group Divisions:
```
Electron Dynamics---------------Torrance, CA
Industrial Products-------------Carlsbad, CA
Connecting Devices------------- * Irvine/Rancho
Santa Margarita
Microelectronic Systems-------- * Irvine/Rancho
Santa Margarita
Solid State Products-----------Newport Beach, CA
Microelectronic Circuits-------Newport Beach, CA
* in Aug- 92 went to Carlsbad, CA
```

Missile Systems Group Divisions:
```
AMRAAM-------------------------Canoga Park, CA
Maverick Division--------------Canoga Park, CA
Missile Development------------Canoga Park, CA
Roland-------------------------Canoga Park, CA
Systems------------------------Canoga Park, CA
Manufacturing------------------Tucson, AZ
```

Radar Systems Group Divisions:
```
Advanced Programs--------------El Segundo, CA
Engineering--------------------El Segundo, CA
Manufacturing------------------El Segundo, CA
Phoenix Systems----------------El Segundo, CA
Aeronautical Operations--------Van Nuys, CA
```

Space & Communications Group Divisions:
```
Commercial Systems-------------El Segundo, CA
Defense Systems----------------El Segundo, CA
NASA Systems-------------------El Segundo, CA
Product Operations-------------El Segundo, CA
Satellite Ground Equipment-----El Segundo, CA
Technology---------------------El Segundo, CA
```

Support Systems Divisions:
```
Field Service & Support--------Long Beach, CA
Test & Training Systems--------Long Beach, CA
```

Research Laboratories Departments:
Chemical Physics----------------Malibu, CA
Electron Device Physics---------Malibu, CA
Exploratory Studies-------------Malibu, CA
High Voltage Technology---------Malibu, CA
Ion Physics---------------------Malibu, CA
Optical Circuits----------------Malibu, CA
Optical Physics-----------------Malibu, CA

International:
Headquaters---------------------Culver City, CA

Major Operating Subsidiaries & Affiliates:
Subsidiaries
AZ Engineering Co---------------Santa Ana, CA
Ensambladores Electronicos de
Mexico--------------------------Mexicali, Mexico
Hughes Aircraft International
Service Company-----------------Culver City, CA
Hughes Aircraft Systems
International--------------------Culver City, CA
Hughes Communication Carrier
Services------------------------El Segundo, CA
Hughes Communication Services---El Segundo, CA
Hughes Communications-----------El Segundo, CA
Hughes Communications
International--------------------El Segundo, CA
Hughes Microelectronics---------Glenrothes, Fife,
Scotland
Santa Barbara Research Center---Goleta, CA
Spectrolab----------------------Sylmar, CA
Affiliates
COMCO Electronics Corp----------Culver City, CA
Elektronik-Und Luftfahrtgerate
GMbH----------------------------Bonn, Germany
Eltro GmbH----------------------Heidelberg, Germany
Eutronic------------------------Brussels, Belgium
HBH Company---------------------Washington, D-C-
Nippon Aviotronics Co-----------Tokyo, Japan
UKADGE Systems------------------London, England

Many people questioned why Hughes Aircraft never entered the medical field. It certainly had the technology. The rumor was that the senior management did not even want the appearance of a conflict of interest. Perhaps I was young but I thought the original Hughes Management was different. In fact I left because outsiders started to come into the organization and pushed aside the Hughes team, or perhaps I was just waking up to reality. In any case, it is a shame because we may have actually had a simpler medical challenge in the USA today if the Hughes Executives applied the massive company resources in this area. There is no question that the medical field missed many technological advances from large system engineering projects after WWII. In many ways they are stuck in a pre WWII era of process and technology application. But that is a different subject.

As I witnessed this enormous event I did not understand it. I had no context. I thought it was irrelevant and the world was a great big place. The WWII generation, at Hughes, came to me and talked yet again, but this time about my environment and what was happening. Their take on the situation was laughter, disbelief and a statement that I will never forget - If they take this place apart they will never be able to recreate it. Boy was that statement ever true and it has haunted me for decades. I will die with that statement reverberating in my head.

Getting back to emergence. It can be good and it can be bad. It can come from technology or from non-technical areas. Be careful what you do because what may emerge is your worst nightmare. Fullerton is now a Raytheon division. So, 23 years of lost technology, 23 years of lost solutions, 23 years of nothing, just like in the movie, the "Never Ending Story".

In this time frame RCA disappeared and Sarnoff lost its funding source. It only exists as a brand name with the original RCA technology powerhouse scattered across various domestic and international companies. AT&T was forced to divest and AT&T Bell labs lost its funding source. Hughes Aircraft disappeared and Hughes Malibu R&D labs lost its funding source. The companies in the USA have no applied R&D budgets. These buckets of money are used to capture projects with funding sources. - *If they take this place apart they will never be able to recreate it. -*

Diversity

The biggest travesty on AAS was not that Hughes Aircraft evaporated or that IBM milked the taxpayer or that Martin Marietta as the oversight contractor failed or that the FAA was blamed when they had no control in the new political setting. The biggest travesty was all the eggs were tossed into one basket in a time when decentralization, smaller government, and empowerment were words used to inspire the advertised coming changes.

Again I was visited by the WWII generation. They said, Walt this is too big it will never fly. I was shocked, yet again. If I could comprehend it and visualize it then it could surely be done this thing called AAS. They would go into huge discussions of politics and the politics of getting a simple RADAR site up and running in a local community. I thought these were silly hollow agreements, the facilities all existed all we had to do was roll in the new equipment and slowly roll out the old equipment.

However, there was something different about the AAS system. AAS was supposed to replace all the command centers. This included all the En-Route, TRACON, and Tower equipment. The idea was to take advantage of commonality and reduce maintenance costs. The previous system had evolved over the decades and it was made up of a plethora of technologies and companies. It was a maintenance nightmare. So the idea was, now that we know how the thing works lets just redo the whole thing with one set of technologies and one company. This will significantly reduce maintenance nightmares plaguing the current system. It made perfect sense to me. I knew this stuff like the back of my hand. I was at the facilities, at the R&D centers, I opened the cabinet doors of the equipment, and I poked around in the details of the circuits, and I helped set up a prototype lab with new generation hardware to do ATC magic. It made sense to me. I thought it would be trivial.

One day at an AAS meeting while I was presenting, someone mentioned that the AAS was larger and more challenging than the Apollo program. It was a person from Sanders, our display contractor. People laughed at the comment. I remember my reaction to this day. I turned my head sideways. I did not laugh I had no reaction. At the time people thought the challenging programs were

Mars probes. Some secretly felt we would see extensive space travel. I guess I was in that category. So in some ways AAS was not taken seriously because of technical arrogance and hubris. But even though I knew more about the system than anyone else did in that room I did not laugh. It was in a time of many arrogant technologists - we called them primadonnas.

Now is time for another WWII one way discussion. Several times various individuals would stop into my office and say Walt, we are so far ahead of everyone else it will take decades for other countries to catch up to where we are today. I now believe we have been surpassed by many of these countries. It only took 20 years of failed policy.

So there is beauty in diversity. Just as a company, technology, or a solution can fail so can policy. The simple policy decision to gather up all the FAA R&D programs into a few huge programs put many companies out of business and placed all the eggs into way too few baskets. It was an act of pure arrogance and hubris and the original comments of this being too big were correct.

Now how does this fit with the decentralization, smaller government, and empowerment words used to inspire the advertised coming changes to fix the problems of the 1970s? It does not; there is the tragedy. Here is a thought experiment. Creativity, innovation, and invention are so unique it takes hundreds of millions of people to surface people with these characteristics in narrow domains like air traffic control. Continue the experiment. What if someone has the arrogance to view this as nothing more than a commodity and they feel they should own it.

During the time frame of AAS there were strong forces to privatize the FAA. The players were IBM, Hughes Aircraft, and MITRE. They each wanted to own the FAA with its trust fund of billions and its cash cow of gate fees. This was an international trend and New Zealand was one of the first air traffic control systems to be privatized. In the past, if you wanted to be an air traffic controller you filled out an application with the government and if you were accepted you were subjected to government training at government labs. You either made it or you washed out. Typically you came from the military and had previous air traffic control training and experience, much like pilots. Your educational qualifications for entry were high school. Today there are associate degrees being offered in air traffic control that you must have to enter the air traffic controller world. What do you do with your associate degree if you don't get accepted into the system? This is just more echo of confusing the roles of commerce, government, non-profits, charity, education and loss of true diversity.

Complexity

The thing about complexity is that it is complex. One of the approaches to deal with complexity is to simplify. The problem is that simplification can come from management, marketing, operations, vested interests, and other inadequate sources. This is not simplification this is stupidly usually "descoping" the complexity or completely missing, not realizing or understanding the complexity. However the approach to complexity is still simplification.

The simplification needs to come from true genius. That is the definition of genius, reducing the complex so that anyone anywhere can understand and deal with what was once thought of as complex and incomprehensible. The problem is that this rails against the concept of replaceable cogs where uniqueness, creativity, innovation, and invention wrapped within real genius are not acknowledged.

That way intellectual property and financial rewards inherent in intellectual property can be effectively managed. It can be managed so well that our modern civilization can collapse as financial dynasties are maintained and true innovators and geniuses are lost or thrown away as commodities. Just because a people may think they have free markets and ownership, it does not mean that the markets are truly free and that ownership is protected. This in many ways was one of the great struggles prior to the rollout of the New Deal in the last century.

So complexity can be reduced. But a simple process or machine can not reduce real complexity. It requires something much more complex and spectacular. It requires humans to do what comes naturally. This means that humans need to be provided an environment where they can live to their fullest potential.

So this is a case where a problem can not be solved with

technology. This is a political social problem, which if addressed can allow genius to flourish and express itself while addressing complexity in all aspects of life.

Communications

Remember my heavy emphasis on key requirements and issues. Well there is a reason for that. At some point things need to be written down and all the stakeholders need to be included in the dialog. Remember the reference to STOP invented at Hughes Aircraft Fullerton in 1962. You can now take your key requirements and issues and address them as a sequence of topics and themes where you tackle each one with the science and engineering you have performed. This is so important because it is a mechanism that tries to codify and implement genius. Remember it takes genius to make the complex simple.

With effective communication using a simple picture, supporting text, with references to the detailed science, everyone can become part of the decision process regardless of background. The communication mechanism itself integrated with the process of key requirements and issue analysis creates the effects of genius. With effective communications, emergence both good and bad is stimulated. This is an extremely powerful technology that needs to be applied to equally challenging problems, as it was in the last century.

Perspectives

Perspectives are so important. My perspective on Sustainable Development is that all our institutions are broken. None of them can handle this challenge in this new century. They have become ineffective in providing real tangible needs of our society. Many people are grossly underemployed sitting in cubicles being directed by bureaucrats; today we call them managers, who are only responding to very narrow vested interests. Much of this is a result of the 1970's when there was a general malaise that something was wrong and productivity was viewed as the cause. The solution was management and control. We now know that was not the case. We now know that it was the start of what is now firmly entrenched, even in our high tech communities.

Bill Gates is worth $40 billion dollars, depending on the market. He has established the largest foundation in the United States, just in front of the Howard Hughes Medical Institute. The endowment of the Howard Hughes Medical Institute was valued at approximately $16 billion in 2007. The endowment of the Bill & Melinda Gates Foundation was valued at approximately $37 billion in 2007. No one questions that Billy Gates controls thousands of high tech workers who could have sprung out of his organization into their own businesses offering creative and innovative high tech solutions outside of Microsoft Windows and Office.

The Howard Hughes Empire did not sink all knowledge and work into one area. The workers engaged in broad research and development and the company responded to requests for help from the government, both defense and non-defense, and from industry. Yes Howard had his pet projects but so did thousands of high tech workers pushing their passions. In fact many stayed to pursue their passions because of the vast resources available within Hughes. This is one of the companies that could take sand and build space ships.

So, $1 billion dollars employs 10,000 people for 1 year or 1,000 people for 10 years. Another way to look at it is that $1 billion dollars will create 20 independently wealthy people with $50 million per person to pursue their high tech passions. Today, these people are stuck in cages with salaries that will not allow them to do the great works that need to be done now and should have been done in the last century. The best way to describe this is a small department at Hughes Aircraft Fullerton chartered with developing air defense and air traffic control displays did everything that Microsoft does, in fact they were part of the group that invented this stuff. These things were a hell of a lot more sophisticated than what Microsoft has done. In fact Microsoft just took the work from people like these as they implemented their windows and word processing applications. So $40 billion dollars could have spawned 800 nicely funded research and development labs.

We had a similar thing happened in the last century where enormous capital was concentrated, I believe it resulted in the great depression. Capital is what a modern economy needs. Creativity comes from people. The more people you have with capital the greater the creativity coming out of the system. Not much creativity can come from a single person no matter how creative they think they are once compared to a dozen people. What does it mean to remove creativity, a natural flowing human characteristic from 1 million people? This is not rocket science; we learned this at the start of the previous century. Oh well. I wonder if anyone will propose divesting some of these new institutions?

There was another company that could take sand and create spectacular things. That was RCA. I used my RCA portable VCR and CCD camera circa 1983, both incredible feats of science and engineering, to record my children as they grew up. This is priceless. I believe they also went to the Moon.

One could argue that we cannot breakup these new dinosaurs because they need to be big enough to compete in the International arena against entities owned by foreign governments. In the 1980's the markets started their internationalized movements. Essentially the world was changed where any foreign entity could invest outside its borders. So now US citizens can buy stock in foreign companies and non-US citizens can by stock in US companies. This seems like a great turn for freedom and liberty unless some large stockholder outside the US starts dictating what they want to do with a company in the US. The same holds true for people outside the US and their national assets.

Media has also changed. Everywhere in public places there is a TV screen with the same Orewellian image of a news channel. In my younger days I was treated to music and television with soap operas, game shows, movies, cartoons, and yes, occasional news but not the same meaningless bullshit over and over in all public places. Technology, in this case the Internet has surfaced with alternative news sources. They have become very popular and they have raised some serious questions in the past few years. These questions should not be pushed aside using management techniques of damage control. This is especially true in the Sustainable Development and Global Warming areas.

Alternative media has made claims that Sustainable Development has a hidden agenda of more draconian social control and loss of freedom. It has even gone so far as to suggest genocide and other methods to reduce population that is no longer sustainable. These claims should be met head on by those involved. They should form the basis of the key requirements and key issues.

So perspectives are important. Be careful whose perspectives you decide to censor. Your children or their children may curse you forever.

Terraforming

Every system has a system heart. Sometimes there are two system hearts. In the case of Air Traffic Control the system hearts are the air traffic controller console and the RADAR tracker running in the computers. There could have been a third heart associated with the introduction of AERA (Automated En Route Air Traffic Control), but that did not happen.

I think the system heart for Sustainable Development is Terraforming. Most people will say it is Energy and specifically petroleum, but I think that is too narrow. It is like talking about the power that feeds an air traffic control system. It is not the heart of the system. Terraforming has its roots in of all places science fiction with some pointing to a science-fiction story published in 1942. I think Carl Sagan bought this to the forefront in his famous TV series "Cosmos". In 1976 NASA addressed the issue of planetary engineering in a study, but used the term planetary ecosynthesis instead.

It was probably 1982, I was in the Hughes Fullerton building 618 courtyard cafeteria having lunch with Fred and some of my age peers. Fred was the Physics professor that basically hired me at Hughes. We were talking about space and planets, a subject that intimidated me. I knew nothing about it when all of the sudden the topic of Mars surfaced and how it is a dead planet. Out of nowhere I just said, well we can fix that. Everyone turned to me in astonishment. I said yea, we can like shove electrodes in at the poles and like engineer, you know create an atmosphere. As my peers were getting ready to roll eyes Fred stepped in and said stuff in a scholarly way. He may have even used the word Terraforming. So don't roll your eyes.

Am I talking about global warming? Yes and no, global warming is too narrow. But let's just look at global warming for now.

The big issue is that our carbon levels are increasing and there is evidence to show that this is leading to a warmer earth. Plants like carbon gas a waste product of animals, automobiles, and industry. Is it possible that we have a scenario of not enough plants on earth? Which plant cleans the atmosphere with the most efficiency? Is it a tree, a blade of grass, a weed, a bush, a flower, a moss, etc. Is it possible to offset the effects of a power generating station with the clever use of plants? Where are the numbers?

This seems like a simple analysis, to measure the conversion rate of plants and determine the degree of care required so that these plants keep growing. Are you aware of the square footage of plants needed to offset your carbon foot print?

Here is a thought experiment. Let's consider what it means to have a Television manufactured in a developing nation versus a destination nation like the USA. What is the carbon footprint of the manufacturing and distribution activities? It would appear that shipping televisions within a country to a seaport for eventual shipment across the ocean would have a larger carbon footprint allocated to the distribution. However, what if we add the worker to the equation. It would appear that the carbon footprint of a worker in a developing nation is smaller than the USA.

But, let us continue with the analysis. What is the potential in terms of creativity, innovation, and invention of a person in a highly stressed social economic setting versus a person who has their basic needs satisfied and may achieve high levels of formal education. One could argue that the well-fed person would squander their wealth and not produce from creativity, innovation, and invention perspectives, but what about the offspring of such a person?

So what does this have to do with Terraforming? This is a tradeoff not unlike deciding the difference between a green moss versus another green thing when attempting to establish another world like Mars. Step 1 is to get some oxygen going. Step 1 in our world today might be to maximize creativity, innovation, and invention so that we can survive. This might be called Human Potential.

So the tradeoff criteria that surfaced from this small thought experiment are Manufacturing, Distribution, Environmental Damage, and Human Potential. The tradeoff might look something like this before science and engineering are applied (3 = best and 1 = worst):

	USA	Dev Nation
Carbon Footprint Manufacturing	2	2
Carbon Footprint Distribution	2	1
Carbon Footprint Human	1	3
Environmental Damage	3	1
Human Potential	3	1
Total	11	8

So the cost to bring a TV to a user in the USA can be 37.5% more costly (11/8) before the benefit starts to shift to the developing nation. Now here is the big issue. Does it make sense for the world and the developing nations to enter into this effort if the process will move the Human Potential up to 3 for the entire planet? If the Human Potential is not permitted to rise, then the investment will be lost.

So Terraforming is not science fiction. We just haven't viewed our challenge from that perspective. Is Terraforming new to humans? No, humans have been doing it on a small scale for a very long time and it began when we went from hunter-gatherers to farmers. In the last century there were huge hydroelectric projects, which had massive impacts on the planet that, we probably never really quantified. We know the changes in the physical and social landscapes, but there were also many other changes.

What a bizarre tradeoff, this is like mixing giraffes with rocks. What do rocks have to do with giraffes? Figures never lie but liar's figure. Remember it is not about the answers it is about the questions. Do I know the right questions? No. But I do know that when the right questions surface the answers become self evident to all reasonable people. Especially if everyone can see and understand the science and engineering and witness the creativity, innovation, and invention.

Does it make sense to turn deserts into green plant growing regions or should we concentrate on existing green regions? Should we even think about massive planetary changes? Do we have the technology to understand the problems and not do more damage than good from our perspective, our ability to thrive? Keep asking the questions my fellow system engineer.

Sustainable Development Project

The proposal is simple. It follows the model of Dr. Vennevar Bushs' seminal work presented to Franklin Roosevelt in the last century. That work is so important that it is included as an Appendix to this book, "Science the Endless Frontier, A Report to the President by Vannevar Bush, Director of the Office of Scientific Research and Development, July 1945".

The program charter is to identify institutions that can take the lead in Sustainable Development using Creative System Engineering. If none exist then propose the structure of such an institution or institutions and how it or they can interact with all other institutions working in this area. The charter also includes where and how Creative System Engineering should be rolled out to existing institutions.

Background

The Brundtland Commission defined sustainable development as development that "meets the needs of the present without compromising the ability of future generations to meet their own needs." Sustainable development is usually divided into social, economic, environmental and institutional. The social, economic, environmental areas address key principles of sustainability, while the institutional area addresses key policy and capacity issues. This is a sample of some of the organizations working in this area:

Renewable Energy: National Renewable Energy Lab, Department of Energy, American Wind Energy Association, Midwest Research Institute, Renewable Energy Systems, General Electric, Battelle

Sustainable Development: Cornell University Center for Sustainable Global Enterprise, National Science Foundation Engineering, University of Michigan Erb Institute for Global Sustainable Enterprise, UC Berkeley Center for Sustainable Resource Development located in the College of Natural Resources,

United Nations Division for Sustainable Development

Terraforming: NASA, Jet Propulsion Lab, NOAA, National Science Foundation Geosciences

This is a sample of some of the organizations that could enter this area and start to make productive contributions:

Other Institutions: Federally Funded Research and Development Centers, Resurrect Hughes Aircraft, Convert Defense Plants engaged in massive System Engineering projects, Foundations, Congressional Committees, Presidential Commissions

Key Requirements

- Allow earth to sustain 100 billion people in next 100 years
- Do not compromise current levels of freedom and liberty
- Uplift all of humanity so all can live to their fullest potential
- Increase the level of bio diversity
- Continue to increase the highest standard of industrial living
- Make the highest industrial standards of living available to anyone desiring such a life style
- Most view these requirements as diametrically opposing, that is the challenge

Key Issues and Observations

- The markets will not solve the problems
- In many ways the markets are the cause of the problem
- There are no impartial institutions that can address the sustainable development problem
- Time is of the urgency, may not be enough time for traditional science Ph.D. thesis
- System engineering using science and engineering may help avert disaster in this century
- Regulation and incentives are not the answer, look to history for guidance
- This is a politically charged area and it should NOT be so
- Humans always did Sustainable Development from step farming to safe water & sewage

Problem Approach

- Prepare major policy paper ala Vannevar Bush letter to President Roosevelt
- Start a literature search of all aspects of sustainable development
- Start a market survey of all sustainable development projects
- Establish a library of the literature search and market survey using the web
- Identify institutions that might be able to take the lead in sustainable development
- Identify the level of impartiality of institutions engaged in sustainable development activities
- Propose a new institution that can take the impartial lead in sustainable development
- Tradeoff new proposed vs. current institutions for sustainable development lead charter
- Establish system engineering centers to perform independent no self interest trade studies

Boundary

- The system boundary can be Earth, USA or Industry
- In this case I recommend the boundary be the USA
- Inputs are Sun, Natural Resources, and Human Mind, Spirit, Creativity, Labor
- Outputs are Food, Clothing, Shelter, Things where humans do not live by bread alone
- Output feeds the Input except the Sun and some Natural Resources
- The goal is to get all Natural Resources to recycle back to the input

It's Too Late What's the Point

Hope springs eternal. It is never too late. The doom and gloom people say the developing countries are quickly rising into first world status. As a result the carbon footprint will cause run away global warming with no way out. Others are saying the planet can only support 8 billion people and really only 2 billion people effectively so 4 billion people will probably kill each other off tomorrow. In all cases it is about our science and technology rising to the occasion. A few hundred years ago our science and technology could only support a few hundred million people on the earth. What happened what changed? How did we get to 6 billion people?

Others talk about urban sprawl as non-stoppable and point to China where their economic progress will soon tip the climate into uncontrollable biblical events. It is ok for science to sound the alarms but it is wrong to think that humans will not rise to the occasion given an opportunity. We now have the opportunity.

I look at my own back yard. Yes I do see people from my generation driving SUVs conveniently forgetting the first energy crisis and the urgent calls for action from that time. But I also see the local auto parts store carry all kinds of recreational vehicles that did not exist just 10 years ago that I could easily use in my commuting if I needed to do so. I happen to live 7 miles from my place of work. I do see people commuting from Northern New Jersey to Southern New Jersey, but that is just a failure of policy. Those that drive north should exchange jobs with those that drive south and all will be much easier. It can be made to happen. I live in a traditional suburb but it was laid out by architects and so there are offices, schools, and shopping sprinkled throughout the community. Public transportation in this setting will work and will be more effective than in any of the old high-density cities of the past like I used live in as a child which were created before any needs for large numbers of people.

Yes there are US communities created in the deregulation days of the 80's and 90's where all the architects and city planners were fired and so they are a mess. Well, that is their problem and they will need to rise to the occasion and add the work centers, shopping, and recreational needs of a healthy community rather than commuting to established healthy communities and causing traffic jams.

The point is the problem has been identified and now it is time for the magic of humans to start. Time to go to work and build the world that will exist in 2100.

Appendix - Dr. Vannevar Bush

I don't know if Vannevar was a devil or a saint. However I do know the words in his famous paper to President Roosevelt contain elements of true altruism and perhaps even love. I also know that this set the policy and tone of the USA after WWII because it would have been impossible for me to have become an engineer and enter the high tech industries in the late 1970's under other conditions.

Are there better examples for this effort than the following from Dr. Vannevar Bush? Probably, but if you don't get his words you probably never will. If enough of you don't get it, then you will go the way of the humans in the film "AI". To be replaced by something you can not comprehend.

Science The Endless Frontier

A Report to the President by Vannevar Bush, Director of the Office of Scientific Research and Development, July 1945

(United States Government Printing Office, Washington: 1945)

Letter Of Transmittal

```
OFFICE OF SCIENTIFIC RESEARCH AND DEVELOPMENT
1530 P Street, NW.
Washington 25, D.C.
JULY 25, 1945
```

DEAR MR. PRESIDENT:

In a letter dated November 17, 1944, President Roosevelt requested my recommendations on the following points:

(1) What can be done, consistent with military security, and with the prior approval of the military authorities, to make known to the world as soon as possible the contributions which have been made during our war effort to scientific knowledge?

(2) With particular reference to the war of science against disease, what can be done now to organize a program for continuing in the future the work which has been done in medicine and related sciences?

(3) What can the Government do now and in the future to aid research activities by public and private organizations?

(4) Can an effective program be proposed for discovering and developing scientific talent in American youth so that the continuing future of scientific research in this country may be assured on a level comparable to what has been done during the war?

It is clear from President Roosevelt's letter that in speaking of science that he had in mind the natural sciences, including biology and medicine, and I have so interpreted his questions. Progress in other fields, such as the social sciences and the humanities, is likewise important; but the program for science presented in my report warrants immediate attention.

In seeking answers to President Roosevelt's questions I have had the assistance of distinguished committees specially qualified to advise in respect to these subjects. The committees have given these matters the serious attention they deserve; indeed, they have regarded this as an opportunity to participate in shaping the policy of the country with reference to scientific research. They have had many meetings and have submitted formal reports. I have been in close touch with the work of the committees and with their members throughout. I have examined all of the data they assembled and the suggestions they submitted on the points raised in President Roosevelt's letter.

Although the report which I submit herewith is my own, the facts, conclusions, and recommendations are based on the findings of the committees which have studied these questions. Since my report is necessarily brief, I am including as appendices the full reports of the committees.

A single mechanism for implementing the recommendations of the several committees is essential. In proposing such a mechanism I have departed somewhat from the specific recommendations of the committees, but I have since been assured that the plan I am proposing is fully acceptable to the committee members.

The pioneer spirit is still vigorous within this nation. Science offers a largely unexplored hinterland for the pioneer who has the tools for his task. The rewards of such exploration both for the Nation and the individual are great. Scientific progress is one essential key to our security as a nation, to our better health, to more jobs, to a higher standard of living, and to our cultural progress.

```
        Respectfully yours,
                              (s) V. Bush, Director

    THE PRESIDENT OF THE UNITED STATES,
    The White House,
    Washington, D. C.

    ___
```

President Roosevelt's Letter

```
THE WHITE HOUSE
Washington, D. C.
November 17, 1944
```

DEAR DR. BUSH: The Office of Scientific Research and Development, of which you are the Director, represents a unique experiment of team-work and cooperation in coordinating scientific research and in applying existing scientific knowledge to the solution of the technical problems paramount in war. Its work has been conducted in the utmost secrecy and carried on without public recognition of any kind; but its tangible results can be found in the communiques coming in from the battlefronts all over the world. Some day the full story of its achievements can be told.

There is, however, no reason why the lessons to be found in this experiment cannot be profitably employed in times of peace. The information, the techniques, and the research experience developed by the Office of Scientific Research and Development and by the thousands of scientists in the universities and in private industry, should be used in the days of peace ahead for the improvement of the national health, the creation of new enterprises bringing new jobs, and the betterment of the national standard of living.

It is with that objective in mind that I would like to have your recommendations on the following four major points:

First: What can be done, consistent with military security, and with the prior approval of the military authorities, to make known to the world as soon as possible the contributions which have been made during our war effort to scientific knowledge?

The diffusion of such knowledge should help us stimulate new enterprises, provide jobs four our returning servicemen and other workers, and make possible great strides for the improvement of the national well-being.

Second: With particular reference to the war of science against disease, what can be done now to organize a program for continuing in the future the work which has been done in medicine and related sciences?

The fact that the annual deaths in this country from one or two diseases alone are far in excess of the total number of lives lost by us in battle during this war should make us conscious of the duty we owe future generations.

Third: What can the Government do now and in the future to aid research activities by public and private organizations? The proper roles of public and of private research, and their interrelation, should be carefully considered.

Fourth: Can an effective program be proposed for discovering and developing scientific talent in American youth so that the continuing future of scientific research in this country may be assured on a level comparable to what has been done during the war?

New frontiers of the mind are before us, and if they are pioneered with the same vision, boldness, and drive with which we have waged this war we can create a fuller and more fruitful employment and a fuller and more fruitful life.

I hope that, after such consultation as you may deem advisable with your associates and others, you can let me have your considered judgment on these matters as soon as convenient - reporting on each when you are ready, rather than waiting for completion of your studies in all.

Very sincerely yours,

(s) FRANKLIN D. ROOSEVELT

Dr. VANNEVAR BUSH,
Office of Scientific Research and Development,
Washington, D. C.

—

Science - The Endless Frontier

"New frontiers of the mind are before us, and if they are pioneered with the same vision, boldness, and drive with which we have waged this war we can create a fuller and more fruitful employment and a fuller and more fruitful life."--

    FRANKLIN D. ROOSEVELT
    November 17, 1944.

――

SUMMARY OF THE REPORT

SCIENTIFIC PROGRESS IS ESSENTIAL

Progress in the war against disease depends upon a flow of new scientific knowledge. New products, new industries, and more jobs require continuous additions to knowledge of the laws of nature, and the application of that knowledge to practical purposes. Similarly, our defense against aggression demands new knowledge so that we can develop new and improved weapons. This essential, new knowledge can be obtained only through basic scientific research.

Science can be effective in the national welfare only as a member of a team, whether the conditions be peace or war. But without scientific progress no amount of achievement in other directions can insure our health, prosperity, and security as a nation in the modern world.

For the War Against Disease

We have taken great strides in the war against disease. The death rate for all diseases in the Army, including overseas forces, has been reduced from 14.1 per thousand in the last war to 0.6 per thousand in this war. In the last 40 years life expectancy has increased from 49 to 65 years, largely as a consequence of the reduction in the death rates of infants and children. But we are far from the goal. The annual deaths from one or two diseases far exceed the total number of American lives lost in battle during this war. A large fraction of these deaths in our civilian population cut short the useful lives of our citizens. Approximately 7,000,000 persons in the United States are mentally ill and their care costs the public over $175,000,000 a year. Clearly much illness remains for which adequate means of prevention and cure are not yet known.

The responsibility for basic research in medicine and the underlying sciences, so essential to progress in the war against disease, falls primarily upon the medical schools and universities. Yet we find that the traditional sources of support for medical research in the medical schools and universities, largely endowment income, foundation grants, and private donations, are diminishing and there is no immediate prospect of a change in this trend. Meanwhile, the cost of medical research has been rising. If we are to maintain the progress in medicine which has marked the last 25 years, the Government should extend financial support to basic medical research in the medical schools and in universities.

For Our National Security

The bitter and dangerous battle against the U-boat was a battle of scientific techniques - and our margin of success was dangerously small. The new eyes which radar has supplied can sometimes be blinded by new scientific developments. V-2 was countered only by capture of the launching sites.

We cannot again rely on our allies to hold off the enemy while we struggle to catch up. There must be more - and more adequate - military research in peacetime. It is essential that the civilian scientists continue in peacetime some portion of those contributions to national security which they have made so effectively during the war. This can best be done through a civilian-controlled organization with close liaison with the Army and Navy, but with funds direct from Congress, and the clear power to initiate military research which will supplement and strengthen that carried on directly under the control of the Army and Navy.

And for the Public Welfare

One of our hopes is that after the war there will be full employment. To reach that goal the full creative and productive energies of the American people must be released. To create more jobs we must make new and better and cheaper products. We want plenty of new, vigorous enterprises. But new products and processes are not born full-grown. They are founded on new principles and new conceptions which in turn result from basic scientific research. Basic scientific research is scientific capital. Moreover, we cannot any longer depend upon Europe as a major source of this scientific capital. Clearly, more and better scientific research is one essential to the achievement of our goal of full employment.

How do we increase this scientific capital? First, we must have plenty of men and women trained in science, for upon them depends both the creation of new knowledge and its application to practical purposes. Second, we must strengthen the centers of basic research which are principally the colleges, universities, and research institutes. These institutions provide the environment which is most conducive to the creation of new scientific knowledge and least under pressure for immediate, tangible results. With some notable exceptions, most research in industry and Government involves application of existing scientific knowledge to practical problems. It is only the colleges, universities, and a few research institutes that devote most of their research efforts to expanding the frontiers of knowledge.

Expenditures for scientific research by industry and Government increased from $140,000,000 in 1930 to $309,000,000 in 1940. Those for the colleges and universities increased from $20,000,000 to $31,000,000, while those for the research institutes declined from $5,200,000 to $4,500,000 during the same period. If the colleges, universities, and research institutes are to meet the rapidly increasing demands of industry and Government for new scientific knowledge, their basic research should be strengthened by use of public funds.

For science to serve as a powerful factor in our national welfare, applied research both in Government and in industry must be vigorous. To improve the quality of scientific research within the Government, steps should be taken to modify the procedures for recruiting, classifying, and compensating scientific personnel in order to reduce the present handicap of governmental scientific bureaus in competing with industry and the universities for top-grade scientific talent. To provide coordination of the common scientific activities of these governmental agencies as to policies and budgets, a permanent Science Advisory Board should be created to advise the executive and legislative branches of Government on these matters.

The most important ways in which the Government can promote industrial research are to increase the flow of new scientific knowledge through support of basic research, and to aid in the development of scientific talent. In addition, the Government should provide suitable incentives to industry to conduct research, (a) by clarification of present uncertainties in the Internal Revenue Code in regard to the deductibility of research and development expenditures as current charges against net income, and (b) by strengthening the patent system so as to eliminate uncertainties which now bear heavily on small industries and so as to prevent abuses which reflect discredit upon a basically sound system. In addition, ways should be found to cause the benefits of basic research to reach industries which do not now utilize new scientific knowledge.

We Must Renew Our Scientific Talent

The responsibility for the creation of new scientific knowledge - and for most of its application - rests on that small body of men and women who understand the fundamental laws of nature and are skilled in the techniques of scientific research. We shall have rapid or slow advance on any scientific frontier depending on the number of highly qualified and trained scientists exploring it.

The deficit of science and technology students who, but for the war, would have received bachelor's degrees is about 150,000. It is estimated that the deficit of those obtaining advanced degrees in these fields will amount in 1955 to about 17,000 - for it takes at least 6 years from college entry to achieve a doctor's degree or its equivalent in science or engineering. The real ceiling on our productivity of new scientific knowledge and its application in the war against disease, and the development of new products and new industries, is the number of trained scientists available.

The training of a scientist is a long and expensive process. Studies clearly show that there are talented individuals in every part of the population, but with few exceptions, those without the means of buying higher education go without it. If ability, and not the circumstance of family fortune, determines who shall receive higher education in science, then we shall be assured of constantly improving quality at every level of scientific activity. The Government should provide a reasonable number of undergraduate scholarships and graduate fellowships in order to develop scientific talent in American youth. The plans should be designed to attract into science only that proportion of youthful talent appropriate to the needs of science in relation to the other needs of the nation for high abilities.

Including Those in Uniform

The most immediate prospect of making up the deficit in scientific personnel is to develop the scientific talent in the generation now in uniform. Even if we should start now to train the current crop of high-school graduates none would complete graduate studies before 1951. The Armed Services should comb their records for men who, prior to or during the war, have given evidence of talent for science, and make prompt arrangements, consistent with current discharge plans, for ordering those who remain in uniform, as soon as militarily possible, to duty at institutions here and overseas where they can continue their scientific education. Moreover, the Services should see that those who study overseas have the benefit of the latest scientific information resulting from research during the war.

THE LID MUST BE LIFTED

While most of the war research has involved the application of existing scientific knowledge to the problems of war, rather than basic research, there has been accumulated a vast amount of information relating to the application of science to particular problems. Much of this can be used by industry. It is also needed for teaching in the colleges and universities here and in the Armed Forces Institutes overseas. Some of this information must remain secret, but most of it should be made public as soon as there is ground for belief that the enemy will not be able to turn it against us in this war. To select that portion which should be made public, to coordinate its release, and definitely to encourage its publication, a

Board composed of Army, Navy, and civilian scientific members should be promptly established.

A PROGRAM FOR ACTION

The Government should accept new responsibilities for promoting the flow of new scientific knowledge and the development of scientific talent in our youth. These responsibilities are the proper concern of the Government, for they vitally affect our health, our jobs, and our national security. It is in keeping also with basic United States policy that the Government should foster the opening of new frontiers and this is the modern way to do it. For many years the Government has wisely supported research in the agricultural colleges and the benefits have been great. The time has come when such support should be extended to other fields.

The effective discharge of these new responsibilities will require the full attention of some over-all agency devoted to that purpose. There is not now in the permanent Governmental structure receiving its funds from Congress an agency adapted to supplementing the support of basic research in the colleges, universities, and research institutes, both in medicine and the natural sciences, adapted to supporting research on new weapons for both Services, or adapted to administering a program of science scholarships and fellowships.

Therefore I recommend that a new agency for these purposes be established. Such an agency should be composed of persons of broad interest and experience, having an understanding of the peculiarities of scientific research and scientific education. It should have stability of funds so that long-range programs may be undertaken. It should recognize that freedom of inquiry must be preserved and should leave internal control of policy, personnel, and the method and scope of research to the institutions in which it is carried on. It should be fully responsible to the President and through him to the Congress for its program.

Early action on these recommendations is imperative if this nation is to meet the challenge of science in the crucial years ahead. On the wisdom with which we bring science to bear in the war against disease, in the creation of new industries, and in the strengthening of our Armed Forces depends in large measure our future as a nation.

Chapter 1 INTRODUCTION

Scientific Progress is Essential

We all know how much the new drug, penicillin, has meant to our grievously wounded men on the grim battlefronts of this war - the countless lives it has saved - the incalculable suffering which its use has prevented. Science and the great practical genius of this nation made this achievement possible.

Some of us know the vital role which radar has played in bringing the United Nations to victory over Nazi Germany and in driving the Japanese steadily back from their island bastions. Again it was painstaking scientific research over many years that made radar possible.

What we often forget are the millions of pay envelopes on a peacetime Saturday night which are filled because new products and new industries have provided jobs for countless Americans. Science made that possible, too.

In 1939 millions of people were employed in industries which did not even exist at the close of the last war - radio, air conditioning, rayon and other synthetic fibers, and plastics are examples of the products of these industries. But these things do not mark the end of progress - they are but the beginning if we make full use of our scientific resources. New manufacturing industries can be started and many older industries greatly strengthened and expanded if we continue to study nature's laws and apply new knowledge to practical purposes.

Great advances in agriculture are also based upon scientific research. Plants which are more resistant to disease and are adapted to short growing season, the prevention and cure of livestock diseases, the control of our insect enemies, better fertilizers, and improved agricultural practices, all stem from painstaking scientific research.

Advances in science when put to practical use mean more jobs, higher wages, shorter hours, more abundant crops, more leisure for recreation, for study, for learning how to live without the deadening drudgery which has been the burden of the common man for ages past. Advances in science will also bring higher standards of living, will lead to the prevention or cure of diseases, will promote conservation of our limited national resources, and will assure means of defense against aggression. But to achieve these objectives - to secure a high level of employment, to maintain a position of world leadership - the flow of new scientific knowledge must be both continuous and substantial.

Our population increased from 75 million to 130 million between 1900 and 1940. In some countries comparable increases have been accompanied by famine. In this country the increase has been accompanied by more abundant food supply, better living, more leisure, longer life, and better health. This is, largely, the product of three factors - the free play of initiative of a vigorous people under democracy, the heritage of great national wealth, and the advance of science and its application.

Science, by itself, provides no panacea for individual, social, and economic ills. It can be effective in the national welfare only as a member of a team, whether the conditions be peace or war. But without scientific progress no amount of achievement in other directions can insure our health, prosperity, and security as a nation in the modern world.

Science Is a Proper Concern of Government

It has been basic United States policy that Government should foster the opening of new frontiers. It opened the seas to clipper ships and furnished land for pioneers. Although these frontiers have more or less disappeared, the frontier of science remains. It is in keeping with the American tradition - one which has made the United States great - that new frontiers shall be made accessible for development by all American citizens.

Moreover, since health, well-being, and security are proper concerns of Government, scientific progress is, and must be, of vital interest to Government. Without scientific progress the national health would deteriorate; without scientific progress we could not hope for improvement in our standard of living or for an increased number of jobs for our citizens; and without scientific progress we could not have maintained our liberties against tyranny.

Government Relations to Science - Past and Future

From early days the Government has taken an active interest in scientific matters. During the nineteenth century the Coast and Geodetic Survey, the Naval Observatory, the Department of Agriculture, and the Geological Survey were established. Through the Land Grant College acts the Government has supported research in state institutions for more than 80 years on a gradually increasing scale. Since 1900 a large number of scientific agencies have been established within the Federal Government, until in 1939 they numbered more than 40.

Much of the scientific research done by Government agencies is intermediate in character between the two types of work commonly referred to as basic and applied research. Almost all Government scientific work has ultimate practical objectives but, in many fields of broad national concern, it commonly involves long-term investigation of a fundamental nature. Generally speaking, the scientific agencies of Government are not so concerned with immediate practical objectives as are the laboratories of industry nor, on the other hand, are they as free to explore any natural phenomena without regard to possible economic applications as are the educational and private research institutions. Government scientific agencies have splendid records of achievement, but they are limited in function.

We have no national policy for science. The Government has only begun to utilize science in the nation's welfare. There is no body within the Government charged with formulating or executing a national science policy. There are no standing committees of the Congress devoted to this important subject. Science has been in the wings. It should be brought to the center of the stage - for in it lies much of our hope for the future.

There are areas of science in which the public interest is acute but which are likely to be cultivated inadequately if left without more support than will come from private sources. These areas - such as research on military problems, agriculture, housing, public health, certain medical research, and research involving expensive capital facilities beyond the capacity of private institutions - should be advanced by active Government support. To date, with the exception of the intensive war research conducted by the Office of Scientific Research and Development, such support has been meager and intermittent.

For reasons presented in this report we are entering a period when science needs and deserves increased support from public funds.

Freedom of Inquiry Must Be Preserved

The publicly and privately supported colleges, universities, and research institutes are the centers of basic research. They are the wellsprings of knowledge and understanding. As long as they are vigorous and healthy and their scientists are free to pursue the truth wherever it may lead, there will be a flow of new scientific knowledge to those who can apply it to practical problems in Government, in industry, or elsewhere.

Many of the lessons learned in the war-time application of science under Government can be profitably applied in peace. The Government is peculiarly fitted to perform certain functions, such as the coordination and support of broad programs on problems of great national importance. But we must proceed with caution in carrying over the methods which work in wartime to the very different conditions of peace. We must remove the rigid controls which we have had to impose, and recover freedom of inquiry and that healthy competitive scientific spirit so necessary for expansion of the frontiers of scientific knowledge.

Scientific progress on a broad front results from the free play of free intellects, working on subjects of their own choice, in the manner dictated by their curiosity for exploration of the unknown. Freedom of inquiry must be preserved under any plan for Government support of science in accordance with the Five Fundamentals listed on page 26.

The study of the momentous questions presented in President Roosevelt's letter has been made by able committees working diligently. This report presents conclusions and recommendations based upon the studies of these committees which appear in full as the appendices. Only in the creation of one over-all mechanism rather than several does this report depart from the specific recommendations of the committees. The members of the committees have reviewed the recommendations in regard to the single mechanism and have found this plan thoroughly acceptable.

Chapter 2 THE WAR AGAINST DISEASE

In War

The death rate for all diseases in the Army, including the overseas forces, has been reduced from 14.1 per thousand in the last war to 0.6 per thousand in this war.

Such ravaging diseases as yellow fever, dysentery, typhus, tetanus, pneumonia, and meningitis have been all but conquered by penicillin and the sulfa drugs, the insecticide DDT, better vaccines, and improved hygenic measures. Malaria has been controlled. There has been dramatic progress in surgery.

The striking advances in medicine during the war have been possible only because we had a large backlog of scientific data accumulated through basic research in many scientific fields in the years before the war.

In Peace

In the last 40 years life expectancy in the United States has increased from 49 to 65 years largely as a consequence of the reduction in the death rates of infants and children; in the last 20 years the death rate from the diseases of childhood has been reduced 87 percent.

Diabetes has been brought under control by insulin, pernicious anemia by liver extracts; and the once widespread deficiency diseases have been much reduced, even in the lowest income groups, by accessory food factors and improvement of diet. Notable advances have been made in the early diagnosis of cancer, and in the surgical and radiation treatment of the disease.

These results have been achieved through a great amount of basic research in medicine and the preclinical sciences, and by the dissemination of this new scientific knowledge through the physicians and medical services and public health agencies of the country. In this cooperative endeavour the pharmaceutical industry has played an important role, especially during the war. All of the medical and public health groups share credit for these achievements; they form interdependent members of a team.

Progress in combating disease depends upon an expanding body of new scientific knowledge.

Unsolved Problems

As President Roosevelt observed, the annual deaths from one or two diseases are far in excess of the total number of American lives lost in battle during this war. A large fraction of these deaths in our civilian population cut short the useful lives of our citizens. This is our present position despite the fact that in the last three decades notable progress has been made in civilian medicine. The reduction in death rate from diseases of childhood has shifted the emphasis to the middle and old age groups, particularly to the malignant diseases and the degenerative processes prominent in later life. Cardiovascular disease, including chronic disease of the kidneys, arteriosclerosis, and cerebral hemorrhage, now account for 45 percent of the deaths in the United States. Second are the infectious diseases, and third is cancer. Added to these are many maladies (for example, the common cold, arthritis, asthma and hay fever, peptic ulcer) which, through infrequently fatal, cause incalculable disability.

Another aspect of the changing emphasis is the increase of mental diseases. Approximately 7 million persons in the United States are mentally ill; more than one-third of the hospital beds are occupied by such persons, at a cost of $175 million a year. Each year 125,000 new mental cases are hospitalized.

Notwithstanding great progress in prolonging the span of life and relief of suffering, much illness remains for which adequate means of prevention and cure are not yet known. While additional physicians, hospitals, and health programs are needed, their full usefulness cannot be attained unless we enlarge our knowledge of the human organism and the nature of disease. Any extension of medical facilities must be accompanied by an expanded program of medical training and research.

Broad and Basic Studies Needed

Discoveries pertinent to medical progress have often come from remote and unexpected sources, and it is certain that this will be true in the future. It is wholly probable that progress in the treatment of cardiovascular disease, renal disease, cancer, and similar refractory diseases will be made as the result of fundamental discoveries in subjects unrelated to those diseases, and perhaps entirely unexpected by the investigator. Further progress requires that the entire front of medicine and the underlying sciences of chemistry, physics, anatomy, biochemistry, physiology, pharmacology, bacteriology, pathology, parasitology, etc., be broadly developed.

Progress in the war against disease results from discoveries in remote and unexpected fields of medicine and the underlying sciences.

Coordinated Attack on Special Problems

Penicillin reached our troops in time to save countless lives because the Government coordinated and supported the program of research and development on the drug. The development moved from the early laboratory stage to large scale production and use in a fraction of the time it would have taken without such leadership. The search for better anti-malarials, which proceeded at a moderate tempo for many years, has been accelerated enormously by Government support during the war. Other examples can be cited in which medical progress has been similarly advanced. In achieving these results, the Government has provided over-all coordination and support; it has not dictated how the work should be done within any cooperating institution.

Discovery of new therapeutic agents and methods usually results from basic studies in medicine and the underlying sciences. The development of such materials and methods to the point at which they become available to medical practitioners requires teamwork involving the medical schools, the science departments of universities, Government and the pharmaceutical industry. Government initiative, support, and coordination can be very effective in this development phase.

Government initiative and support for the development of newly discovered therapeutic materials and methods can reduce the time required to bring the benefits to the public.

Action is Necessary

The primary place for medical research is in the medical schools and universities. In some cases coordinated direct attack on special problems may be made by teams of investigators, supplementing similar attacks carried on by the Army, Navy, Public Health Service, and other organizations. Apart from teaching, however, the primary obligation of the medical schools and universities is to continue the traditional function of such institutions, namely, to provide the individual worker with an opportunity for free, untrammeled study of nature, in the directions and by the methods suggested by his interests, curiosity, and imagination. The history of medical science teaches clearly the supreme importance of affording the prepared mind complete freedom for the exercise of initiative. It is the special province of the medical schools and universities to foster medical research in this way - a duty which cannot be shifted to government agencies, industrial organizations, or to any other institutions.

Where clinical investigations of the human body are required, the medical schools are in a unique position, because of their close relationship to teaching hospitals, to integrate such investigations with the work of the departments of preclinical science, and to impart new knowledge to physicians in training. At the same time, the teaching hospitals are especially well qualified to carry on medical research because of their close connection with the medical schools, on which they depend for staff and supervision.

Between World War I and World War II the United States overtook all other nations in medical research and assumed a position of world leadership. To a considerable extent this progress reflected the liberal financial support from university endowment income, gifts from individuals, and foundation grants in the 20's. The growth of research departments in medical schools ahs been very uneven, however, and in consequence most of the important work has been done in a few large schools. This should be corrected by building up the weaker institutions, especially in regions which now have no strong medical research activities.

The traditional sources of support for medical research, largely endowment income, foundation grants, and private donations, are diminishing, and there is no immediate prospect of a change in this trend. Meanwhile, research costs have steadily risen. More elaborate and expensive equipment is required, supplies are more costly, and the wages of assistants are higher. Industry is only to a limited extent a source of funds for basic medical research.

It is clear that if we are to maintain the progress in medicine which has marked the last 25 years, the Government should extend financial support to basic medical research in the medical schools and in the universities, through grants both for research and for fellowships. The amount which can be effectively spent in the first year should not exceed 5 million dollars. After a program is under way perhaps 20 million dollars a year can be spent effectively.

Chapter 3 SCIENCE AND THE PUBLIC WELFARE

Relation to National Security

In this war it has become clear beyond all doubt that scientific research is absolutely essential to national security. The bitter and dangerous battle against the U-boat was a battle of scientific techniques - and our margin of success was dangerously small. The new eyes which radar supplied to our fighting forces quickly evoked the development of scientific countermeasures which could often blind them. This again represents the ever continuing battle of techniques. The V-1 attack on London was finally defeated by three devices developed during this war and used superbly in the field. V-2 was countered only by the capture of the launching sites.

The Secretaries of War and Navy recently stated in a joint letter to the National Academy of Sciences:

This war emphasizes three facts of supreme importance to national security: (1) Powerful new tactics of defense and offense are developed around new weapons created by scientific and engineering research; (2) the competitive time element in developing those weapons and tactics may be decisive; (3) war is increasingly total war, in which the armed services must be supplemented by active participation of every element of civilian population.

To insure continued preparedness along farsighted technical lines, the research scientists of the country must be called upon to continue in peacetime some substantial portion of those types of contribution to national security which they have made so effectively during the stress of the present war * * *.

There must be more - and more adequate - military research during peacetime. We cannot again rely on our allies to hold off the enemy while we struggle to catch up. Further, it is clear that only the Government can undertake military research; for it must be carried on in secret, much of it has no commercial value, and it is expensive. The obligation of Government to support research on military problems is inescapable.

Modern war requires the use of the most advanced scientific techniques. Many of the leaders in the development of radar are scientists who before the war had been exploring the nucleus of the atom. While there must be increased emphasis on science in the future training of officers for both the Army and Navy, such men cannot be expected to be specialists in scientific research. Therefore a professional partnership between the officers in the Services and civilian scientists is needed.

The Army and Navy should continue to carry on research and development on the improvement of current weapons. For many years the National Advisory Committee for Aeronautics has supplemented the work of the Army and Navy by conducting basic research on the problems of flight. There should now be permanent civilian activity to supplement the research work of the Services in other scientific fields so as to carry on in time of peace some part of the activities of the emergency war-time Office of Scientific Research and Development.

Military preparedness requires a permanent independent, civilian-controlled organization, having close liaison with the Army and Navy, but with funds directly from Congress and with the clear power to initiate military research which will supplement and strengthen that carried on directly under the control of the Army and Navy.

Military preparedness requires a permanent independent, civilian-controlled organization, having close liaison with the Army and Navy, but with funds directly from Congress and with the clear power to initiate military research which will supplement and strengthen that carried on directly under the control of the Army and Navy.

Science and Jobs

One of our hopes is that after the war there will be full employment, and that the production of goods and services will serve to raise our standard of living. We do not know yet how we shall reach that goal, but it is certain that it can be achieved only by releasing the full creative and productive energies of the American people.

Surely we will not get there by standing still, merely by making the same things we made before and selling them at the same or higher prices. We will not get ahead in international trade unless we offer new and more attractive and cheaper products.

Where will these new products come from? How will we find ways to make better products at lower cost? The answer is clear. There must be a stream of new scientific knowledge to turn the wheels of private and public enterprise. There must be plenty of men and women trained in science and technology for upon them depend both the creation of new knowledge and its application to practical purposes.

More and better scientific research is essential to the achievement of our goal of full employment.

The Importance of Basic Research

Basic research is performed without thought of practical ends. It results in general knowledge and an understanding of nature and its laws. This general knowledge provides the means of answering a large number of important practical problems, though it may not give a complete specific answer to any one of them. The function of applied research is to provide such complete answers. The scientist doing basic research may not be at all interested in the practical applications of his work, yet the further progress of industrial development would eventually stagnate if basic scientific research were long neglected.

One of the peculiarities of basic science is the variety of paths which lead to productive advance. Many of the most important discoveries have come as a result of experiments undertaken with very different purposes in mind. Statistically it is certain that important and highly useful discoveries will result from some fraction of the undertakings in basic science; but the results of any one particular investigation cannot be predicted with accuracy.

Basic research leads to new knowledge. It provides scientific capital. It creates the fund from which the practical applications of knowledge must be drawn. New products and new processes do not appear full-grown. They are founded on new principles and new conceptions, which in turn are painstakingly developed by research in the purest realms of science.

Today, it is truer than ever that basic research is the pacemaker of technological progress. In the nineteenth century, Yankee mechanical ingenuity, building largely upon the basic discoveries of European scientists, could greatly advance the technical arts. Now the situation is different.

A nation which depends upon others for its new basic scientific knowledge will be slow in its industrial progress and weak in its competitive position in world trade, regardless of its mechanical skill.

Centers of Basic Research

Publicly and privately supported colleges and universities and the endowed research institutes must furnish both the new scientific knowledge and the trained research workers. These institutions are uniquely qualified by tradition and by their special characteristics to carry on basic research. They are charged with the responsibility of conserving the knowledge accumulated by the past, imparting that knowledge to students, and contributing new knowledge of all kinds. It is chiefly in these institutions that scientists may work in an atmosphere which is relatively free from the adverse pressure of convention, prejudice, or commercial necessity. At their best they provide the scientific worker with a strong sense of solidarity and security, as well as a substantial degree of personal intellectual freedom. All of these factors are of great importance in the development of new knowledge, since much of new knowledge is certain to arouse opposition because of its tendency to challenge current beliefs or practice.

Industry is generally inhibited by preconceived goals, by its own clearly defined standards, and by the constant pressure of commercial necessity. Satisfactory progress in basic science seldom occurs under conditions prevailing in the normal industrial laboratory. There are some notable exceptions, it is true, but even in such cases it is rarely possible to match the universities in respect to the freedom which is so important to scientific discovery.

To serve effectively as the centers of basic research these institutions must be strong and healthy. They must attract our best scientists as teachers and investigators. They must offer research opportunities and sufficient compensation to enable them to compete with industry and government for the cream of scientific talent.

During the past 25 years there has been a great increase in industrial research involving the application of scientific knowledge to a multitude of practical purposes - thus providing new products, new industries, new investment opportunities, and millions of jobs. During the same period research within Government - again largely applied research - has also been greatly expanded. In the decade from 1930 to 1940 expenditures for industrial research increased from $116,000,000 to $240,000,000 and those for scientific research in Government rose from $24,000,000 to $69,000,000. During the same period expenditures for scientific research in the colleges and universities increased from $20,000,000 to $31,000,000, while those in the endowed research institutes declined from $5,200,000 to $4,500,000. These are the best estimates available. The figures have been taken from a variety of sources and arbitrary definitions have necessarily been applied, but it is believed that they may be accepted as indicating the following trends:

- (a) Expenditures for scientific research by industry and Government - almost entirely applied research - have more than doubled between 1930 and 1940. Whereas in 1930 they were six times as large as the research expenditures of the colleges, universities, and research institutes, by 1940 they were nearly ten times as large.
- (b) While expenditures for scientific research in the colleges and universities increased by one-half during this period, those for the endowed research institutes have slowly declined.

If the colleges, universities, and research institutes are to meet the rapidly increasing demands of industry and Government for new scientific knowledge, their basic research should be strengthened by use of public funds.

Research Within the Government

Although there are some notable exceptions, most research conducted within governmental laboratories is of an applied nature. This has always been true and is likely to remain so. Hence Government, like industry, is dependent on the colleges, universities, and research institutes to expand the basic scientific frontiers and to furnish trained scientific investigators.

Research within the Government represents an important part of our total research activity and needs to be strengthened and expanded after the war. Such expansion should be directed to fields of inquiry and service which are of public importance and are not adequately carried on by private organizations.

The most important single factor in scientific and technical work is the quality of the personnel employed. The procedures currently followed within the Government for recruiting, classifying and compensating such personnel place the Government under a severe handicap in competing with industry and the universities for first-class scientific talent. Steps should be taken to reduce that handicap.

In the Government the arrangement whereby the numerous scientific agencies form parts of larger departments has both advantages and disadvantages. but the present pattern is firmly established and there is much to be said for it. There is, however, a very real need for some measure of coordination of the common scientific activities of these agencies, both as to policies and budgets, and at present no such means exist.

A permanent Science Advisory Board should be created to consult with these scientific bureaus and to advise the executive and legislative branches of Government as to the policies and budgets of Government agencies engaged in scientific research.

This board should be composed of disinterested scientists who have no connection with the affairs of any Government agency.

Industrial Research

The simplest and most effective way in which the Government can strengthen industrial research is to support basic research and to develop scientific talent.

The benefits of basic research do not reach all industries equally or at the same speed. Some small enterprises never receive any of the benefits. It has been suggested that the benefits might be better utilized if "research clinics" for such enterprises were to be established. Businessmen would thus be able to make more use of research than they now do. This proposal is certainly worthy of further study.

One of the most important factors affecting the amount of industrial research is the income-tax law. Government action in respect to this subject will affect the rate of technical progress in industry. Uncertainties as to the attitude of the Bureau of Internal Revenue regarding the deduction of research and development expenses are a deterrent to research expenditure. These uncertainties arise from lack of clarity of the tax law as to the proper treatment of such costs.

The Internal Revenue Code should be amended to remove present uncertainties in regard to the deductibility of research and development expenditures as current charges against net income.

Research is also affected by the patent laws. They stimulate new invention and they make it possible for new industries to be built around new devices or new processes. These industries generate new jobs and new products, all of which contribute to the welfare and the strength of the country.

Yet, uncertainties in the operation of the patent laws have impaired the ability of small industries to translate new ideas into processes and products of value to the nation. These uncertainties are, in part, attributable to the difficulties and expense incident to the operation of the patent system as it presently exists. These uncertainties are also attributable to the existence of certain abuses, which have appeared in the use of patents. The abuses should be corrected. They have led to extravagantly critical attacks which tend to discredit a basically sound system.

It is important that the patent system continue to serve the country in the manner intended by the Constitution, for it has been a vital element in the industrial vigor which has distinguished this nation.

The National Patent Planning Commission has reported on this subject. In addition, a detailed study, with recommendations concerning the extent to which modifications should be made in our patent laws is currently being made under the leadership of the Secretary of Commerce. It is recommended, therefore, that specific action with regard to the patent laws be withheld pending the submission of the report devoted exclusively to that subject.

International Exchange of Scientific Information

International exchange of scientific information is of growing importance. Increasing specialization of science will make it more important than ever that scientists in this country keep continually ahead of developments abroad. In addition a flow of scientific information constitutes one facet of general international accord which should be cultivated.

The Government can accomplish significant results in several ways: by aiding in the arrangement of international science congresses, in the official accrediting of American scientists to such gatherings, in the official reception of foreign scientists of standing in this country, in making possible a rapid flow of technical information, including translation service, and possibly in the provision of international fellowships. Private foundations and other groups partially fulfill some of these functions at present, but their scope is incomplete and inadequate.

The Government should take an active role in promoting the international flow of scientific information.

The Special Need for Federal Support

We can no longer count on ravaged Europe as a source of fundamental knowledge. In the past we have devoted much of our best efforts to the application of such knowledge which has been discovered abroad. In the future we must pay increased attention to discovering this knowledge for ourselves particularly since the scientific applications of the future will be more than ever dependent upon such basic knowledge.

New impetus must be given to research in our country. Such impetus can come promptly only from the Government. Expenditures for research in the colleges, universities, and research institutes will otherwise not be able to meet the additional demands of increased public need for research.

Further, we cannot expect industry adequately to fill the gap. Industry will fully rise to the challenge of applying new knowledge to new products. The commercial incentive can be relied upon for that. But basic research is essentially noncommercial in nature. It will not receive the attention it requires if left to industry.

For many years the Government has wisely supported research in the agricultural colleges and the benefits have been great. The time has come when such support should be extended to other fields.

In providing government support, however, we must endeavor to preserve as far as possible the private support of research both in industry and in the colleges, universities, and research institutes. These private sources should continue to carry their share of the financial burden.

The Cost of a Program

It is estimated that an adequate program for Federal support of basic research in the colleges, universities, and research institutes and for financing important applied research in the public interest, will cost about 10 million dollars at the outset and may rise to about 50 million dollars annually when fully underway at the end of perhaps 5 years.

Chapter 4 RENEWAL OF OUR SCIENTIFIC TALENT

Nature of the Problem

The responsibility for the creation of new scientific knowledge rests on that small body of men and women who understand the fundamental laws of nature and are skilled in the techniques of scientific research. While there will always be the rare individual who will rise to the top without benefit of formal education and training, he is the exception and even he might make a more notable contribution if he had the benefit of the best education we have to offer. I cannot improve on President Conant's statement that:

"* * * in every section of the entire area where the word science may properly be applied, the limiting factor is a human one. We shall have rapid or slow advance in this direction or in that depending on the number of really first-class men who are engaged in the work in question. * * * So in the last analysis, the future of science in this country will be determined by our basic educational policy."

A Note of Warning

It would be folly to set up a program under which research in the natural sciences and medicine was expanded at the cost of the social sciences, humanities, and other studies so essential to national well-being. This point has been well stated by the Moe Committee as follows:

" As citizens, as good citizens, we therefore think that we must have in mind while examining the question before us - the discovery and development of scientific talent - the needs of the whole national welfare. We could not suggest to you a program which would syphon into science and technology a disproportionately large share of the nation's highest abilities, without doing harm to the nation, nor, indeed, without crippling science. * * * Science cannot live by and unto itself alone."

       *   *   *   *   *   *   *   *

"The uses to which high ability in youth can be put are various and, to a large extent, are determined by social pressures and rewards. When aided by selective devices for picking out scientifically talented youth, it is clear that large sums of money for scholarships and fellowships and monetary and other rewards in disproportionate amounts might draw into science too large a percentage of the nation's high ability, with a result highly detrimental to the nation and to science. Plans for the discovery and development of scientific talent must be related to the other needs of society for high ability. * * * There is never enough ability at high levels to satisfy all the needs of the nation; we would not seek to draw into science any more of it than science's proportionate share."

The Wartime Deficit

Among the young men and women qualified to take up scientific work, since 1940 there have been few students over 18, except some in medicine and engineering in Army and Navy programs and a few 4-F's, who have followed an integrated scientific course of studies. Neither our allies nor, so far as we know, our enemies have done anything so radical as thus to suspend almost completely their educational activities in scientific pursuits during the war period.

Two great principles have guided us in this country as we have turned our full efforts to war. First, the sound democratic principle that there should be no favored classes or special privilege in a time of peril, that all should be ready to sacrifice equally; second, the tenet that every man should serve in the capacity in which his talents and experience can best be applied for the prosecution of the war effort. In general we have held these principles well in balance.

In my opinion, however, we have drawn too heavily for nonscientific purposes upon the great natural resource which resides in our trained young scientists and engineers. For the general good of the country too many such men have gone into uniform, and their talents have not always been fully utilized. With the exception of those men engaged in war research, all physically fit students at graduate level have been taken into the armed forces. Those ready for college training in the sciences have not been permitted to enter upon that training.

There is thus an accumulating deficit of trained research personnel which will continue for many years. The deficit of science and technology students who, but for the war, would have received bachelor's degrees is about 150,000. The deficit of those holding advanced degrees - that is, young scholars trained to the point where they are capable of carrying on original work - has been estimated as amounting to about 17,000 by 1955 in chemistry, engineering, geology, mathematics, physics, psychology, and the biological sciences.

With mounting demands for scientists both for teaching and for research, we will enter the post-war period with a serious deficit in our trained scientific personnel.

Improve the Quality

Confronted with these deficits, we are compelled to look to the use of our basic human resources and formulate a program which will assure their conservation and effective development. The committee advising me on scientific personnel has stated the following principle which should guide our planning:

"If we were all-knowing and all-wise we might, but we think probably not, write you a plan whereby there might be selected for training, which they otherwise would not get, those who, 20 years hence, would be scientific leaders, and we might not bother about any lesser manifestations of scientific ability. But in the present state of knowledge a plan cannot be made which will select, and assist, only those young men and women who will give the top future leadership to science. To get top leadership there must be a relatively large base of high ability selected for development and then successive skimmings of the cream of ability at successive times and at higher levels. No one can select from the bottom those who will be the leaders at the top because unmeasured and unknown factors enter into scientific, or any, leadership. There are brains and character, strength and health, happiness and spiritual vitality, interest and motivation, and no one knows what else, that must needs enter into this supra-mathematical calculus.

"We think we probably would not, even if we were all-wise and all-knowing, write you a plan whereby you would be assured of scientific leadership at one stroke. We think as we think because we are not interested in setting up an elect. We think it much the best plan, in this constitutional Republic, that opportunity be held out to all kinds and conditions of men whereby they can better themselves. This is the American way; this is the way the United States has become what it is. We think it very important that circumstances be such that there be no ceilings, other than ability itself, to intellectual ambition. We think it very important that every boy and girl shall know that, if he shows that he has what it takes, the sky is the limit. Even if it be shown subsequently that he has not what it takes to go to the top, he will go further than he would otherwise go if there had been a ceiling beyond which he always knew he could not aspire.

"By proceeding from point to point and taking stock on the way, by giving further opportunity to those who show themselves worthy of further opportunity, by giving the most opportunity to those who show themselves continually developing - this is the way we propose. This is the American way: a man work for what he gets."

Remove the Barriers

Higher education in this country is largely for those who have the means. If those who have the means coincided entirely with those persons who have the talent we should not be squandering a part of our higher education on those undeserving of it, nor neglecting great talent among those who fail to attend college for economic reasons. There are talented individuals in every segment of the population, but with few exceptions those without the means of buying higher education go without it. Here is a tremendous waste of the greatest resource of a nation - the intelligence of its citizens.

If ability, and not the circumstance of family fortune, is made to determine who shall receive higher education in science, then we shall be assured of constantly improving quality at every level of scientific activity.

The Generation in Uniform Must Not Be Lost

We have a serious deficit in scientific personnel partly because the men who would have studied science in the colleges and universities have been serving in the Armed Forces. Many had begun their studies before they went to war. Others with capacity for scientific education went to war after finishing high school. The most immediate prospect of making up some of the deficit in scientific personnel is by salvaging scientific talent from the generation in uniform. For even if we should start now to train the current crop of high school graduates, it would be 1951 before they would complete graduate studies and be prepared for effective scientific research. This fact underlines the necessity of salvaging potential scientists in uniform.

The Armed Services should comb their records for men who, prior to or during the war, have given evidence of talent for science, and make prompt arrangements, consistent with current discharge plans, for ordering those who remain in uniform as soon as militarily possible to duty at institutions here and overseas where they can continue their scientific education. Moreover, they should see that those who study overseas have the benefit of the latest scientific developments.

A Program

The country may be proud of the fact that 95 percent of boys and girls of the fifth grade age are enrolled in school, but the drop in enrollment after the fifth grade is less satisfying. For every 1,000 students in the fifth grade, 600 are lost to education before the end of high school, and all but 72 have ceased formal education before completion of college. While we are concerned primarily with methods of selecting and educating high school graduates at the college and higher levels, we cannot be complacent about the loss of potential talent which is inherent in the present situation.

Students drop out of school, college, and graduate school, or do not get that far, for a variety of reasons: they cannot afford to go on; schools and colleges providing courses equal to their capacity are not available locally; business and industry recruit many of the most promising before they have finished the training of which they are capable. These reasons apply with particular force to science: the road is long and expensive; it extends at least 6 years beyond high school; the percentage of science students who can obtain first-rate training in institutions near home is small.

Improvement in the teaching of science is imperative; for students of latent scientific ability are particularly vulnerable to high school teaching which fails to awaken interest or to provide adequate instruction. To enlarge the group of specially qualified men and women it is necessary to increase the number who go to college. This involves improved high school instruction, provision for helping individual talented students to finish high school (primarily the responsibility of the local communities), and opportunities for more capable, promising high school students to go to college. Anything short of this means serious waste of higher education and neglect of human resources.

To encourage and enable a larger number of young men and women of ability to take up science as a career, and in order gradually to reduce the deficit of trained scientific personnel, it is recommended that provision be made for a reasonable number of (a) undergraduate scholarships and graduate fellowships and (b) fellowships for advanced training and fundamental research. The details should be worked out with reference to the interests of the several States and of the universities and colleges; and care should be taken not to impair the freedom of the institutions and individuals concerned.

The program proposed by the Moe Committee in Appendix 4 would provide 24,000 undergraduate scholarships and 900 graduate fellowships and would cost about $30,000,000 annually when in full operation. Each year under this program 6,000 undergraduate scholarships would be made available to high school graduates, and 300 graduate fellowships would be offered to college graduates. Approximately the scale of allowances provided for under the educational program for returning veterans has been used in estimating the cost of this program.

The plan is, further, that all those who receive such scholarships or fellowships in science should be enrolled in a National Science Reserve and be liable to call into the service of the Government, in connection with scientific or technical work in time of war or other national emergency declared by Congress or proclaimed by the President. Thus, in addition to the general benefits to the nation by reason of the addition to its trained ranks of such a corps of scientific workers, there would be a definite benefit to the nation in having these scientific workers on call in national emergencies. The Government would be well advised to invest the money involved in this plan even if the benefits to the nation were thought of solely - which they are not - in terms of national preparedness.

Chapter 5 A PROBLEM OF SCIENTIFIC RECONVERSION

Effects of Mobilization of Science for War

We have been living on our fat. For more than 5 years many of our scientists have been fighting the war in the laboratories, in the factories and shops, and at the front. We have been directing the energies of our scientists to the development of weapons and materials and methods, on a large number of relatively narrow projects initiated and controlled by the Office of Scientific Research and Development and other Government agencies. Like troops, the scientists have been mobilized, and thrown into action to serve their country in time of emergency. But they have been diverted to a greater extent than is generally appreciated from the search for answers to the fundamental problems - from the search on which human welfare and progress depends. This is not a complaint - it is a fact. The mobilization of science behind the lines is aiding the fighting men at the front to win the war and to shorten it; and it has resulted incidentally in the accumulation of a vast amount of experience and knowledge of the application of science to particular problems, much of which can be put to use when the war is over. Fortunately, this country had the scientists - and the time - to make this contribution and thus to advance the date of victory.

Security Restrictions Should Be Lifted Promptly

Much of the information and experience acquired during the war is confined to the agencies that gathered it. Except to the extent that military security dictates otherwise, such knowledge should be spread upon the record for the benefit of the general public.

Thanks to the wise provision of the Secretary of War and the Secretary of the Navy, most of the results of war-time medical research have been published. Several hundred articles have appeared in the professional journals; many are in process of publication. The material still subject to security classification should be released as soon as possible.

It is my view that most of the remainder of the classified scientific material should be released as soon as there is ground for belief that the enemy will not be able to turn it against us in this war. Most of the information needed by industry and in education can be released without disclosing its embodiments in actual military material and devices. Basically there is no reason to believe that scientists of other countries will not in time rediscover everything we now know which is held in secrecy. A broad dissemination of scientific information upon which further advances can readily be made furnishes a sounder foundation for our national security than a policy of restriction which would impede our own progress although imposed in the hope that possible enemies would not catch up with us.

During the war it has been necessary for selected groups of scientists to work on specialized problems, with relatively little information as to what other groups were doing and had done. Working against time, the Office of Scientific Research and Development has been obliged to enforce this practice during the war, although it was realized by all concerned that it was an emergency measure which prevented the continuous cross-fertilization so essential to fruitful scientific effort.

Our ability to overcome possible future enemies depends upon scientific advances which will proceed more rapidly with diffusion of knowledge than under a policy of continued restriction of knowledge now in our possession.

Need for Coordination

In planning the release of scientific data and experience collected in connection with the war, we must not overlook the fact that research has gone forward under many auspices - the Army, the Navy, the Office of Scientific Research and Development, the National Advisory Committee for Aeronautics, other departments and agencies of the Government, educational institutions, and many industrial organizations. There have been numerous cases of independent discovery of the same truth in different places. To permit the release of information by one agency and to continue to restrict it elsewhere would be unfair in its effect and would tend to impair the morale and efficiency of scientists who have submerged individual interests in the controls and restrictions of war.

A part of the information now classified which should be released is possessed jointly by our allies and ourselves. Plans for release of such information should be coordinated with our allies to minimize danger of international friction which would result from sporadic uncontrolled release.

A Board to Control Release

The agency responsible for recommending the release of information from military classification should be an Army, Navy, civilian body, well grounded in science and technology. It should be competent to advise the Secretary of War and the Secretary of the Navy. It should, moreover, have sufficient recognition to secure prompt and practical decisions.

To satisfy these considerations I recommend the establishment of a Board, made up equally of scientists and military men, whose function would be to pass upon the declassification and to control the release for publication of scientific information which is now classified.

Publication Should Be Encouraged

The release of information from security regulations is but one phase of the problem. The other is to provide for preparation of the material and its publication in a form and at a price which will facilitate dissemination and use. In the case of the Office of Scientific Research and Development, arrangements have been made for the preparation of manuscripts, while the staffs under our control are still assembled and in possession of the records, as soon as the pressure for production of results for this war has begun to relax.

We should get this scientific material to scientists everywhere with great promptness, and at as low a price as is consistent with suitable format. We should also get it to the men studying overseas so that they will know what has happened in their absence.

It is recommended that measures which will encourage and facilitate the preparation and publication of reports be adopted forthwith by all agencies, governmental and private, possessing scientific information released from security control.

Chapter 6 THE MEANS TO THE END

New Responsibilities for Government

One lesson is clear from the reports of the several committees attached as appendices. The Federal Government should accept new responsibilities for promoting the creation of new scientific knowledge and the development of scientific talent in our youth.

The extent and nature of these new responsibilities are set forth in detail in the reports of the committees whose recommendations in this regard are fully endorsed.

In discharging these responsibilities Federal funds should be made available. We have given much thought to the question of how plans for the use of Federal funds may be arranged so that such funds will not drive out of the picture funds from local governments, foundations, and private donors. We believe that our proposals will minimize that effect, but we do not think that it can be completely avoided. We submit, however, that the nation's need for more and better scientific research is such that the risk must be accepted.

It is also clear that the effective discharge of these responsibilities will require the full attention of some over-all agency devoted to that purpose. There should be a focal point within the Government for a concerted program of assisting scientific research conducted outside of Government. Such an agency should furnish the funds needed to support basic research in the colleges and universities, should coordinate where possible research programs on matters of utmost importance to the national welfare, should formulate a national policy for the Government toward science, should sponsor the interchange of scientific information among scientists and laboratories both in this country and abroad, and should ensure that the incentives to research in industry and the universities are maintained. All of the committees advising on these matters agree on the necessity for such an agency.

The Mechanism

There are within Government departments many groups whose interests are primarily those of scientific research. Notable examples are found within the Departments of Agriculture, Commerce, Interior, and the Federal Security Agency. These groups are concerned with science as collateral and peripheral to the major problems of those Departments. These groups should remain where they are, and continue to perform their present functions, including the support of agricultural research by grants to the Land Grant Colleges and Experiment Stations, since their largest contribution lies in applying fundamental knowledge to the special problems of the Departments within which they are established.

By the same token these groups cannot be made the repository of the new and large responsibilities in science which belong to the Government and which the Government should accept. The recommendations in this report which relate to research within the Government, to the release of scientific information, to clarification of the tax laws, and to the recovery and development of our scientific talent now in uniform can be implemented by action within the existing structure of the Government. But nowhere in the Governmental structure receiving its funds from Congress is there an agency adapted to supplementing the support of basic research in the universities, both in medicine and the natural sciences; adapted to supporting research on new weapons for both Services; or adapted to administering a program of science scholarships and fellowships.

A new agency should be established, therefore, by the Congress for the purpose. Such an agency, moreover, should be an independent agency devoted to the support of scientific research and advanced scientific education alone. Industry learned many years ago that basic research cannot often be fruitfully conducted as an adjunct to or a subdivision of an operating agency or department. Operating agencies have immediate operating goals and are under constant pressure to produce in a tangible way, for that is the test of their value. None of these conditions is favorable to basic research. research is the exploration of the unknown and is necessarily speculative. It is inhibited by conventional approaches, traditions, and standards. It cannot be satisfactorily conducted in an atmosphere where it is gauged and tested by operating or production standards. Basic scientific research should not, therefore, be placed under an operating agency whose paramount concern is anything other than research. Research will always suffer when put in competition with operations. The decision that there should be a new and independent agency was reached by each of the committees advising in these matters.

I am convinced that these new functions should be centered in one agency. Science is fundamentally a unitary thing. The number of independent agencies should be kept to a minimum. Much medical progress, for example, will come from fundamental advances in chemistry. Separation of the sciences in tight compartments, as would occur if more than one agency were involved, would retard and not advance scientific knowledge as a whole.

Five Fundamentals

There are certain basic principles which must underlie the program of Government support for scientific research and education if such support is to be effective and if it is to avoid impairing the very things we seek to foster. These principles are as follows:

(1) Whatever the extent of support may be, there must be stability of funds over a period of years so that long-range programs may be undertaken. (2) The agency to administer such funds should be composed of citizens selected only on the basis of their interest in and capacity to promote the work of the agency. They should be persons of broad interest in and understanding of the peculiarities of scientific research and education. (3) The agency should promote research through contracts or grants to organizations outside the Federal Government. It should not operate any laboratories of its own. (4) Support of basic research in the public and private colleges, universities, and research institutes must leave the internal control of policy, personnel, and the method and scope of the research to the institutions themselves. This is of the utmost importance. (5) While assuring complete independence and freedom for the nature, scope, and methodology of research carried on in the institutions receiving public funds, and while retaining discretion in the allocation of funds among such institutions, the Foundation proposed herein must be responsible to the President and the Congress. Only through such responsibility can we maintain the proper relationship between science and other aspects of a democratic system. The usual controls of audits, reports, budgeting, and the like, should, of course, apply to the administrative and fiscal operations of the Foundation, subject, however, to such adjustments in procedure as are necessary to meet the special requirements of research.

Basic research is a long-term process - it ceases to be basic if immediate results are expected on short-term support. Methods should therefore be found which will permit the agency to make commitments of funds from current appropriations for programs of five years duration or longer. Continuity and stability of the program and its support may be expected (a) from the growing realization by the Congress of the benefits to the public from scientific research, and (b) from the conviction which will grow among those who conduct research under the auspices of the agency that good quality work will be followed by continuing support.

Military Research

As stated earlier in this report, military preparedness requires a permanent, independent, civilian-controlled organization, having close liaison with the Army and Navy, but with funds direct from Congress and the clear power to initiate military research which will supplement and strengthen that carried on directly under the control of the Army and Navy. As a temporary measure the National Academy of Sciences has established the Research Board for National Security at the request of the Secretary of War and the Secretary of the Navy. This is highly desirable in order that there may be no interruption in the relations between scientists and military men after the emergency wartime Office of Scientific Research and Development goes out of existence. The Congress is now considering legislation to provide funds for this Board by direct appropriation.

I believe that, as a permanent measure, it would be appropriate to add to the agency needed to perform the other functions recommended in this report the responsibilities for civilian-initiated and civilian-controlled military research. The function of such a civilian group would be primarily to conduct long-range scientific research on military problems - leaving to the Services research on the improvement of existing weapons.

Some research on military problems should be conducted, in time of peace as well as in war, by civilians independently of the military establishment. It is the primary responsibility of the Army and Navy to train the men, make available the weapons, and employ the strategy that will bring victory in combat. The Armed Services cannot be expected to be experts in all of the complicated fields which make it possible for a great nation to fight successfully in total war. There are certain kinds of research - such as research on the improvement of existing weapons - which can best be done within the military establishment. However, the job of long-range research involving application of the newest scientific discoveries to military needs should be the responsibility of those civilian scientists in the universities and in industry who are best trained to discharge it thoroughly and successfully. It is essential that both kinds of research go forward and that there be the closest liaison between the two groups.

Placing the civilian military research function in the proposed agency would bring it into close relationship with a broad program of basic research in both the natural sciences and medicine. A balance between military and other research could thus readily be maintained.

The establishment of the new agency, including a civilian military research group, should not be delayed by the existence of the Research Board for National Security, which is a temporary measure. Nor should the creation of the new agency be delayed by uncertainties in regard to the postwar organization of our military departments themselves. Clearly, the new agency, including a civilian military research group within it, can remain sufficiently flexible to adapt its operations to whatever may be the final organization of the military departments.

National Research Foundation

It is my judgment that the national interest in scientific research and scientific education can best be promoted by the creation of a National Research Foundation.

I. Purposes. - The National Research Foundation should develop and promote a national policy for scientific research and scientific education, should support basic research in nonprofit organizations, should develop scientific talent in American youth by means of scholarships and fellowships, and should by contract and otherwise support long-range research on military matters.

II. Members. - 1. Responsibility to the people, through the President and Congress, should be placed in the hands of, say nine Members, who should be persons not otherwise connected with the Government and not representative of any special interest, who should be known as National Research Foundation Members, selected by the President on the basis of their interest in and capacity to promote the purposes of the Foundation.

2. The terms of the Members should be, say, 4 years, and no Member should be eligible for immediate reappointment provided he has served a full 4-year term. It should be arranged that the Members first appointed serve terms of such length that at least two Members are appointed each succeeding year.

3. The Members should serve without compensation but should be entitled to their expenses incurred in the performance of their duties.

4. The Members should elect their own chairman annually.

5. The chief executive officer of the Foundation should be a director appointed by the Members. Subject to the direction and supervision of the Foundation Members (acting as a board), the director should discharge all the fiscal, legal, and administrative functions of the Foundation. The director should receive a salary that is fully adequate to attract an outstanding man to the post.

6. There should be an administrative office responsible to the director to handle in one place the fiscal, legal, personnel, and other similar administrative functions necessary to the accomplishment of the purposes of the Foundation.

7. With the exception of the director, the division members, and one executive officer appointed by the director to administer the affairs of each division, all employees of the Foundation should be appointed under Civil Service regulations.

III. Organization. - 1. In order to accomplish the purposes of the Foundation the Members should establish several professional Divisions to be responsible to the Members. At the outset these Divisions should be:

a. Division of Medical Research. - The function of this Division should be to support medical research.

b. Division of Natural Sciences. - The function of this Division should be to support research in the physical and natural sciences.

c. Division of National Defense. - It should be the function of this Division to support long-range scientific research on military matters.

d. Division of Scientific Personnel and Education. - It should be the function of this Division to support and to supervise the grant of scholarships and fellowships in science.

e. Division of Publications and Scientific Collaboration. - This Division should be charged with encouraging the publication of scientific knowledge and promoting international exchange of scientific information.

2. Each Division of the Foundation should be made up of at least five members, appointed by the Members of the Foundation. In making such appointments the Members should request and consider recommendations from the National Academy of Sciences which should be asked to establish a new National Research Foundation nominating committee in order to bring together the

recommendations of scientists in all organizations. The chairman of each Division should be appointed by the Members of the Foundation.

3. The division Members should be appointed for such terms as the Members of the Foundation may determine, and may be reappointed at the discretion of the Members. They should receive their expenses and compensation for their services at a per diem rate of, say, $50 while engaged on business of the Foundation, but no division member should receive more than, say, $10,000 compensation per year.

4. Membership of the Division of National Defense should include, in addition to, say, five civilian members, one representative designated by the Secretary of War, and one representative of the Secretary of the Navy, who should serve without additional compensation for this duty.

```
=================================================================
        Proposed Organization of National Research Foundation
                 ================================
                 | National Research Foundation |
                 |------------------------------|
                 |            Members           |
                 ================================
                              |
                     ----------------------
                     |      Director       |
                     ----------------------
                              |
                              |--------------------
                              |                   |
                              |       --------------------------
                              |       | Staff offices           |
                              |       | General Counsel         |
                              |       | Finance Officer         |
                              |       | Administrative planning |
                              |       | Personnel               |
                              |       --------------------------
                              |
---------------------------------------------------------------------
Div of        Div of        Div of      Div of      Div of
Medical       Scientific    Natural     National    Publications
Research      Personnel &   Sciences    Defense     & Scientific
              Education                              Collaboration
--------      --------      --------    --------     --------
Members       Members       Members     Members      Members
--------      --------      --------    --------     --------
Exec. Off.    Exec. Off.    Exec. Off.  Exec. Off.  Exec. Off.
--------      --------      --------    --------     --------
=================================================================
```

IV. Functions. - 1. The Members of the Foundation should have the following functions, powers, and duties:

a. To formulate over-all policies of the Foundation.

b. To establish and maintain such offices within the United States, its territories and possessions, as they may deem necessary.

c. To meet and function at any place within the United States, its territories and possessions.

d. To obtain and utilize the services of other Government agencies to the extent that such agencies are prepared to render such services.

e. To adopt, promulgate, amend, and rescind rules and regulations to carry out the provisions of the legislation and the policies and practices of the Foundation.

f. To review and balance the financial requirements of the several Divisions and to propose to the President the annual estimate for the funds required by each Division. Appropriations should be earmarked for the purposes of specific Divisions, but the Foundation should be left discretion with respect to the expenditure of each Division's funds.

g. To make contracts or grants for the conduct of research by negotiation without advertising for bids.

And with the advice of the National Research Foundation Divisions concerned -

h. To create such advisory and cooperating agencies and councils, state, regional, or national, as in their judgment will aid in effectuating the purposes of the legislation, and to pay the expenses thereof.

i. To enter into contracts with or make grants to educational and nonprofit research institutions for support of scientific research.

j. To initiate and finance in appropriate agencies, institutions, or organizations, research on problems related to the national defense.

k. To initiate and finance in appropriate organizations research projects for which existing facilities are unavailable or inadequate.

l. To establish scholarships and fellowships in the natural sciences including biology and medicine.

m. To promote the dissemination of scientific and technical information and to further its international exchange.

n. To support international cooperation in science by providing financial aid for international meetings, associations of scientific societies, and scientific research programs organized on an international basis.

o. To devise and promote the use of methods of improving the transition between research and its practical application in industry.

2. The Divisions should be responsible to the Members of the Foundation for -

a. Formulation of programs and policy within the scope of the particular Divisions.

b. Recommendations regarding the allocation of research programs among research organizations.

c. Recommendation of appropriate arrangements between the Foundation and the organizations selected to carry on the program.

d. Recommendation of arrangements with State and local authorities in regard to cooperation in a program of science scholarships and fellowships.

e. Periodic review of the quality of research being conducted under the auspices of the particular Division and revision of the program of support of research.

f. Presentation of budgets of financial needs for the work of the Division.

g. Maintaining liaison with other scientific research agencies, both governmental and private, concerned with the work of the Division.

V. Patent Policy. - The success of the National Research Foundation in promoting scientific research in this country will depend to a very large degree upon the cooperation of organizations outside the Government. In making contracts with or grants to such organizations the Foundation should protect the public interest adequately and at the same time leave the cooperating organization with adequate freedom and incentive to conduct scientific research. The public interest will normally be adequately protected if the Government receives a royalty-free license for governmental purposes under any patents resulting from work financed by the Foundation. There should be no obligation on the research institution to patent discoveries made as a result of support from the Foundation. There should certainly not be any absolute requirement that all rights in such discoveries be assigned to the Government, but it should be left to the discretion of the director and the interested Division whether in special cases the public interest requires such an assignment. Legislation on this point should leave to the Members of the Foundation discretion as to its patent policy in order that patent arrangements may be adjusted as circumstances and the public interest require.

VI. Special Authority. - In order to insure that men of great competence and experience may be designated as Members of the Foundation and as members of the several professional Divisions, the legislation creating the Foundation should contain specific authorization so that the Members of the Foundation and the Members of the Divisions may also engage in private and gainful employment, notwithstanding the provisions of any other laws: provided, however, that no compensation for such employment is received in any form from any profit-making institution which receives funds under contract, or otherwise, from the Division or Divisions of the Foundation with which the individual is concerned. In normal times, in view of the restrictive statutory prohibitions against dual interests on the part of Government officials, it would be virtually impossible to persuade persons having private employment of any kind to serve the Government in an official capacity. In order, however, to secure the part-time services of the most competent men as Members of the Foundation and the Divisions, these stringent prohibitions should be relaxed to the extent indicated.

Since research is unlike the procurement of standardized items, which are susceptible to competitive bidding on fixed specifications, the legislation creating the National Research Foundation should free the Foundation from the obligation to place its contracts for research through advertising for bids. This is particularly so since the measure of a successful research contract lies not in the dollar cost but in the qualitative and quantitative contribution which is made to our knowledge. The extent of this contribution in turn depends on the creative spirit and talent which can be brought to bear within a research laboratory. The National Research Foundation must, therefore, be free to place its research contracts or grants not only with those institutions which have a demonstrated research capacity but also with other institutions whose latent talent or creative atmosphere affords promise of research success.

As in the case of the research sponsored during the war by the Office of Scientific Research and Development, the research sponsored by the National Research Foundation should be conducted, in general, on an actual cost basis without profit to the institution receiving the research contract or grant.

There is one other matter which requires special mention. Since research does not fall within the category of normal commercial or procurement operations which are easily covered by the usual contractual relations, it is essential that certain statutory and regulatory fiscal requirements be waived in the case of research contractors. For example, the National Research Foundation should be authorized by legislation to make, modify, or amend contracts of all kinds with or without legal consideration, and without performance bonds. Similarly, advance payments should be allowed in the discretion of the Director of the Foundation when required. Finally, the normal vouchering requirements of the General Accounting Office with respect to detailed itemization or substantiation of vouchers submitted under cost contracts should be relaxed for research contractors. Adherence to the usual procedures in the case of research contracts will impair the efficiency of research operations and will needlessly increase the cost of the work of the Government. Without the broad authority along these lines which was contained in the First War Powers Act and its implementing Executive Orders, together with the special relaxation of vouchering requirements granted by the General Accounting Office, the Office of Scientific Research and Development would have been gravely handicapped in carrying on research on military matters during this war. Colleges and universities in which research will be conducted principally under contract with the Foundation are, unlike commercial institutions, not equipped to handle the detailed vouchering procedures and auditing technicalities which are required of the usual Government contractors.

VII. Budget. - Studies by the several committees provide a partial basis for making an estimate of the order of magnitude of the funds required to implement the proposed program. Clearly the program should grow in a healthy manner from modest beginnings. The following very rough estimates are given for the first year of operation after the Foundation is organized and operating, and for the fifth year of operation when it is expected that the operations would have reached a fairly stable level:

Activity	Millions of dollars	
	First year	5th yr
Division of Medical Research	5.0	20.0
Division of Natural Sciences	10.0	50.0
Division of National Defense	10.0	20.0
Div of Scientific Personnel and Education	7.0	29.0
Div of Pubs & Scientific Collaboration	.5	1.0
Administration	1.0	2.5

Action by Congress

The National Research Foundation herein proposed meets the urgent need of the days ahead. The form of the organization suggested is the result of considerable deliberation. The form is important. The very successful pattern of organization of the National Advisory Committee for Aeronautics, which has promoted basic research on problems of flight during the past thirty years, has been carefully considered in proposing the method of appointment of Members of the Foundation and in defining their responsibilities. Moreover, whatever program is established it is vitally important that it satisfy the Five Fundamentals.

The Foundation here proposed has been described only in outline. The excellent reports of the committees which studied these matters are attached as appendices. They will be of aid in furnishing detailed suggestions.

Legislation is necessary. It should be drafted with great care. Early action is imperative, however, if this nation is to meet the challenge of science and fully utilize the potentialities of science. On the wisdom with which we bring science to bear against the problems of the coming years depends in large measure our future as a nation.

About The Cover

The cover is made of two photographs taken almost 30 years apart. The blue sky and clouds picture was taken in Las Vegas Nevada in 2007. The Philadelphia Art Museum and Water Works picture was taken in 1979. These photographs were not staged and were taken at random. In both cases the unusual beauty of the scene attracted me.

The Philadelphia Water Works was the first water treatment facility in the United States. It was a model for all future water works to follow in the New World. People would flock from around the planet to see this facility which combined engineering and art to solve a massive problem of safe water for the inhabitants of Philadelphia. It was born of necessity as the people decided they would not tolerate yet another yellow fever outbreak. The Museum sits on top of the original water reservoir that provided the city with water. As Philadelphia grew the reservoir and Water Works could no longer meet the needs of the city and new projects eventually replaced this once great technological and artistic achievement. It stopped operations in 1909. When I took the picture I knew nothing of the Water Works or its history. Like many things in our world it was invisible to me, until now. I only knew of its beauty in a very urban landscape setting.

When I took the blue sky and clouds photograph, the Nevada sky was unbelievably dark blue with a tinge of puffy clouds and devoid of air pollution or desert dust. Below the blue sky is a city landscape that I cropped out of the picture. It was on a rather attractive pedestrian skywalk linking two massive hotel structures. It remains to be seen how that city and sky will change in the next 100 years.

Bibliography

Film

1. "Never Ending Story", Director: Wolfgang Petersen, Writers: Wolfgang Petersen (screenplay) Herman Weigel (screenplay) Michael Ende (novel) Robert Easton (additional dialogue), 1984
2. "Flashdance", Director: Adrian Lyne, Writers: Tom Hedley and Joe Eszterhas, 1983
3. "1984", Director: Michael Radford, Writers: George Orwell (novel) Michael Radford, 1984
4. "The Island of Dr Mareau", Director: Erle C. Kenton, Writers: H.G. Wells (novel "The Island of Dr. Moreau") Waldemar Young (screenplay) Philip Wylie (screenplay), 1932
5. "Red River", Directors: Howard Hawks, Arthur Rosson (co-director), Writers: Borden Chase (Saturday Evening Post story) Borden Chase (screenplay) & Charles Schnee (screenplay), 1948
6. "An Inconvenient Truth", Director: Davis Guggenheim, 2006
7. "AI", Director: Steven Spielberg, Writers: (WGA) Brian Aldiss (short story "Supertoys Last All Summer Long") Ian Watson (screen story) Steven Spielberg (screenplay), 2001

Television

8. "Twilight Zone", Creator: Rod Sterling, 1959-1964
9. "Connections", BBC, Director: Mick Jackson, Writer: James Burke, 1978
10. "Gulliver's Travels", Director: Charles Sturridge, Writers: Simon Moore (writer) Jonathan Swift (novel), 1996
11. "Dr. Who", BBC, Creator: Sydney Newman, 1963-2008
12. "Dark Skies", Directors: Lou Antonio, Steve Beers and others, Writers: Steve Aspis, David Black, others, 1996-1997
13. "COSMOS", Carl Sagan, Director: Adrian Malone, Writer: Ann Druyan, 1980
14. "Hitch Hikers Guide to the Galaxy", BBC, 1981

Music

15. "Renaissance", full collection, 1972-1979
16. "Beatles", full collection, 1962-1970

Theatre
17. "Les Misérables", Victor Hugo Broadway Musical Adaptation, Original Broadway Cast Audio CD, 1987

Books
18. "Zen and the Art of Motorcycle Maintenance", Robert M. Pirsig
19. "On Bullshit", Princeton professor Harry G. Frankfurt, 2005
20. "The Memorabilia" by Xenophon, 431 BC
21. "The Magical Number plus or minus seven", George Miller Psych. Rev., 63, 2, 56, 81-96, 1956
22. "STOP How to Achieve Coherence in Proposals and Reports", J.R. Tracey, D.E. Rugh, W.S. Starkey, Hughes Aircraft Fullerton California, 1965

Internet
23. Various links: Wikipedia, National Science Foundation, Defense Technical Information Center

Government
24. "Green Paper A European Strategy for Sustainable, Competitive and Secure Energy", Commission Of The European Communities, COM(2006) 105 final, {SEC(2006) 317}, 2006
25. "Stern Review: The Economics of Climate Change", Nicholas Stern, 2006, Paperback 2007
26. "US Climate Change Technology Program Strategic Plan", U.S. Department of Energy (Lead-Agency) 2006
27. "Advanced Automation System (AAS) Request for Proposal", Federal Aviation Administration, DFTA01-83-R-21135, 1983
28. "Technical Development Plan for a Discrete Address Beacon System (DABS)", MIT Lexington Lincoln Lab, 1971
29. "Preliminary Computer Sizing Estimates for Automated En Route ATC (AERA)", MITRE, 1979
30. "Letter Of Transmittal", Vannevar Bush 1945
31. "President Roosevelt's Letter", President Roosevelt, 1944
32. "Science The Endless Frontier, A Report to the President", Vannevar Bush, Director of the Office of Scientific Research and Development, July 1945